LEARNING
THE VALLEY

LEARNING
THE VALLEY

Excursions into the
Shenandoah Valley

JOHN LELAND

The University of South Carolina Press

Published by the University of South Carolina Press
Columbia, South Carolina 29208

www.sc.edu/uscpress

Manufactured in the United States of America

19 18 17 16 15 14 13 12 11 10   10 9 8 7 6 5 4 3 2 1

Library of Congress Cataloging-in-Publication Data

Leland, John, 1950–
    Learning the valley : excursions into the Shenandoah Valley / John Leland.
    p. cm.
    Includes bibliographical references and index.
    ISBN 978-1-57003-913-3 (cloth : alk. paper)
    1. Shenandoah River Valley (Va. and W. Va.)—Description and travel.
    2. Natural history--Shenandoah River Valley (Va. and W. Va.)
    3. Leland, John, 1950– —Travel—Shenandoah River Valley (Va. and W. Va.)
    I. Title.
    F232.S5L45 2010
    917.55'904—dc22

                                                                      2010002602

This book was printed on Glatfelter Natures, a recycled paper with 30 percent postconsumer
waste content.

Contents

Illustrations

Preface

I have spent twenty-five years living in Rockbridge County, Virginia, the natural wonders of which are so manifold and marvelous that a lifetime would not suffice to know them all. For the past thirteen years, my son, Edward, and I have tramped and hiked and biked and canoed the rivers, caves, mountains, woods, and fields of this place he calls home but in which I will always be a visitor, my own childhood—fifty years earlier and five hundred miles farther south—spent on a coastal plain that bears little resemblance to the Shenandoah Valley's open fields and forested mountains. Just as my father took me into the woods and waters of the place we called home, so I take my child, and together we build memories I hope will bind him to me when I, like my father, am buried in the earth we shared with our children. These essays are my reflections on some of the things Edward and I have discovered in our years together, discoveries made before us by the countless others who preceded us in this land and whose accumulated wisdom I have poached in my attempts to better understand this place I find myself in. The essays are intended primarily for my son, who, busy with his own version of his life, remembers these things, if at all, differently than I do. I hope that reading these essays will bring him pleasure in later years. I hope too that they will inspire whoever else reads them to learn the land they live in so that they know they need not travel farther than their own back yards to witness nature's marvels.

Acknowledgments

I wish to thank Alice Ireland and Cheves Leland for reading an early version of the manuscript and making excellent suggestions; the patient and helpful staff at Preston Library of the Virginia Military Institute for their assistance, especially Diane Jacob and Mary Kludy of the archives, who helped me find nineteenth-century texts and illustrations; Colonel Keith Gibson of the Virginia Military Institute Museum for his help with William Washington's paintings; Alice Ireland for graciously letting me copy her painting and Jeremy Ledbetter of Andre's Studio in Lexington for his help in copying it; Alexander Moore of the University of South Carolina Press for yet again sticking his neck out. I also thank my patient editor, Karen Rood, at the press; and my son, Edward, for being Edward, and for whom I wrote and to whom I dedicate this book.

SUGAR CREEK

All maps—the county, topo, geological—agree that here, right here, in this leaf-strewn, dry-as-dust rock rut runs Sugar Creek. But here there is only rock without water, a stone bed lumpier and dustier than mine at home. The Balls, who pretend to live alongside Sugar Creek, remember when the creek rose and ran here and they feared for their basement. But that flood, raised by a hurricane, receded more quickly than Noah's, and within two days Sugar Creek had left its assigned bed to wander where it would. Over the hill and through the woods, a good quarter of a mile away, lies a field where you can sit and hear the creek tumbling cobbles ten feet below the ground. And if you're of a mind, as I have been, you can trace the subterranean course of Sugar Creek back toward its origin on House Mountain's flanks, sneaking, like it, without permission under fence and through field, ear bent to wherever the none-too-level ground sinks and, through dirt and stone, overhear the secret course of Sugar Creek.

Well who hasn't dreamed of trading beds? What we call adultery in humans, geologists call disappearing streams. And in karst country like the Shenandoah Valley, they're as common as roving humans. Once upon a time Sugar Creek was loyal to its chosen course and slept happily in the bed many suppose still calls to it. But at some point a sinkhole lured it into the depths, and slipping its narrow bed, now dry and cracked as last year's snake skin, the creek slithered down between the cobbles to bathe in undiscovered country, surrounded with stalagmites dreaming heavenward and stalactites heavy with desire, dripping from ceilings worn wafer thin, pillowed and sheeted in flowstone, hidden behind draperies of stone. To me abandoned above ground, the creek pulses, faint as a lover's heartbeat overheard through blouse or shirt, its course beneath the skin of earth I tread as secret as the blood's beneath a lover's skin.

Like human philanderers, wandering streams seldom keep their secrets. Collapsing caves reveal their subterranean mysteries in the jumble of a sinkhole, where stalagmite, stalactite, flowstone, and drapery lie broken and dull in the light of day, their mystery eroding, the chaos of their collapse disappearing as rain rounds the stones' broken edges and the earth buries what remains. Geologists as prurient as gossips intent on telling you the escapades of every wayward relative decipher the tangled marriages, divorces, and remarriages of streams captured, stolen, pirated, and disappeared.

From them we learn the sordid truth behind the Blue Ridge's ragged profile. The Potomac, James, and Roanoke rivers run through water gaps in the Blue Ridge. Scattered in between are wind gaps, notches lower than the prevailing three-thousand-foot height of the Blue Ridge, through which rivers to the east once flowed before their headwaters, seduced by the Shenandoah River, the "Beautiful Daughter of the Stars," turned west and north. Manassas Gap, where Interstate 66 crosses the Blue Ridge, is the lowest of Virginia's wind gaps at 850 feet. Swift Run Gap, 2,365 feet high where the Rapidan River fails to pierce the Blue Ridge, bears like a bitter ex-wife the name of her faithless spouse who long ago ran off with the Shenandoah. Farther south still, Rockfish Gap, where Interstate 64 crosses the Blue Ridge at nineteen thousand feet, overlooks South River, philandering north toward the seductive South Fork of the Shenandoah. Closer to home, the Natural Bridge of Virginia rises indignant over Cedar Creek, who seduced the waters of Poague Run to run away with it through an underground tunnel whose sole surviving bit is the two-hundred-foot-high bridge.

These philandering streams wear their infidelities openly. Not so Sugar Creek, preferring to hide as best it can its cheat. No geologist has ever glimpsed the creek's hidden boudoir, guess though they may its nature by comparison to less circumspect streams that carve their ways through open caves. Some even make money off their buried lives—Dixie, Endless, Luray, and Natural Bridge Caverns but four who lay themselves bare for passersby to marvel at their mysteries. We also pay spelunking shrinks good money to inspect the muddy relics of hearts we ourselves have tried to capture or steal in our day. Imagine their job, hour after hour, day after day, listening to us fondle, Gollum-like, our precious, precious memories. Better they than those we betrayed. For who hasn't, insomniac at 3:00 A.M., wondered whatever happened to old what's her name? I've never been quite drunk enough to do what some do—call up at an ungodly hour a long-lost love and thus confirm her wisdom in having dumped me years earlier. But there are nights I wonder if she too remembers. Does Sugar Creek also remember with regret her abandoned bed? And does her bed yearn yet for her return? It's only a creek, Leland. You may think the sound of water coursing over cobbles sings of a buried life, but water's water and rock's but rock. And would my heart were as hard.

The sinkhole behind the Balls' home fills with water after a really good rain, and then, where wild turkey and I have trod, mallards swim. The temporary lake ponds up against a rock ridge thirty feet high, through which the buried creek must trace a tunnel as strait and narrow as the Bible's, flood waters waiting days to pass through to the other side. And once there, where do they go? For downstream of the ridge, the ground is silent. Here there is only dry stone and no sound of water. Farther down valley, flanking John Jordan's old toll road, the farmstead stands where it does because water cold and sweet as an unfaithful spouse's kiss springs boldly out of the ground. And Sugar Creek rejoins the bed cartographers trace in blue ink on their maps, behaving like a good creek should, flowing overground where you can see it and, in spring and summer, dangle your toes in its water and chase the minnows down the limestone rock ledges toward Effinger. Here the creek has carved a narrow valley, open fields on one side and cedar forest on the other. Whoever owns the land has not yet chopped it up into farmettes, so that a walk here is a trip back in time, the narrow roadbed following the creek, which follows its proper bed, the cows happily eating grass and shitting into the spring where I get my watercress and mint, and a noisy kingfisher patrolling what he obviously supposes to be his creek. And who downstream, the creek now keeping to its narrow bed, guesses its hidden life?

⁂ ROCK CRYSTALS

Although it is tempting to look at the forest around us as we hike House Mountain, Edward and I have eyes only for the ground, seeking the glint of sun against stone. We are hunting crystals.

We have a treasure trove at home, Edward having a pack-rat personality and a loose definition of crystal. Anything quartz will do, so that we have bags of what, to me, are unpromising rocks little different from what you might buy at your local garden center but which are, Edward assured me when we gathered them, precious crystal.

We slowly climb the trail, scuffing the leaves and peering at every glint. Fragments of glass, mostly, but now and then, quartz, often as not the broken tip of a long-vanished crystal, milky with impurities and fraught with fracture lines, worth keeping, of course, but not what we are really after. That is six-sided prisms clear as ice. When we first hunted, I'd spy a crystal and call Edward over to search the area around my feet, guiding his impatient glances here, there, and everywhere until he'd see it and yell, "Look, Daddy, look—a crystal!" But now his youthful eyes find more crystals than my old ones, so that I enjoy his joy in finding these melted remains of long-vanished beaches.

Little House Mountain's spectacular summit is a warren of eroded sandstone, carved over time into a maze well worth wasting an afternoon exploring. But what to a hiker seems huge is but a half mile long and only several hundred feet wide, a small purple lozenge on geological maps lost in the pink sea of the Martinsburg Formation that forms House Mountain's massive flanks. Named after Martinsburg, West Virginia, where it was first scientifically described, the formation's several thousand feet of shale and limestone were laid down more than four hundred million years ago, offshore of vanished mountains then rising to the east of today's Shenandoah Valley. As the mountains eroded, the sediments changed from easily weathered particles to purer and purer erosion-resistant quartz, which today makes up the capstones of Little and Big House Mountains.

What today's sun warms was warmed millions of years ago by the earth itself, the Martinsburg's eroding limestones and shales having been buried by geologists only know how many thousands of feet of now-vanished sediments. But deep enough to have melted silicon, which, combined with oxygen, forms silicon dioxide, or quartz. And silicon dioxide sometimes decides to make itself into six-sided prisms tipped with pyramids at either end, although such perfect crystals are rare, most being multiple, distorted, and often clouded, opaque, or milky. But a surprising number of House Mountain's crystals are perfectly clear, six-sided rock crystals.

Before Edward began carrying much of House Mountain home with him, back when I hunted alone, a morning's search might yield a handful of crystals. Off to Lexington jeweler Mr. Hess I would go with my bag of crystals, and we would sort them, discarding this one and that one, seeking the crystal perfect enough for my thirteen-year-old daughter's neck, or two twinned beauties to dangle from her ears. Mr. Hess never made much money off my crystals, but I know he enjoyed our mornings together, telling me of his youth when, he swore, the newly tilled cornfields sparkled with crystals ready for the picking. Today's duller world raises cattle, not corn, when it farms at all, and a Rockbridge County kid is more apt to find crystal in a suburban excavation than a field. But Kathy Ball still tills the earth by hand, and she once gave me as an engagement present a pink-tinged beauty of a stone she had plowed up in her garden, a stony miracle, twinned crystals married forever. My marriage proved less durable than nature's, and I no longer gaze upon that crystal or the woman I thought it represented. Nor does my daughter, Isabella, still wear the crystals I hunted her, having found stones more precious in her sight than those. But they remain, gathering dust in the corner of her jewelry chest. And who knows, perhaps one day her daughter's daughter will discover them, and lift them from the surrounding tangle of store-bought jewelry and learn of a man she never knew who gave her grandmother frozen ice.

For such the Roman naturalist Pliny thought quartz crystals were, the word *crystal* coming from the Greek for ice. The Bible also thought crystal special, Ezekiel's four beasts supporting a firmament "the color of the terrible crystal," while Revelation's "sea of glass" was "like unto crystal." Edgar Cayce reported that Atlantis was powered by giant crystals, one of which still lies in the heart of the Bermuda Triangle. Native Americans also favored crystals, archeologists having discovered they traded them throughout what is now the Southeastern United States. Europeans were also attracted to the stones, and stone churches in south-west Virginia include large, seven-inch-long crystals in their walls. And once upon a not so long time ago, such crystals were the stuff of national security.

Nineteenth-century scientists confirmed earlier research that suggested certain materials, including quartz, generate an electric charge when stressed. This piezoelectricity, from the Greek for *squeeze* or *press*, created a demand for flawless quartz crystals that could be cut and used in sonar, phonograph, and radio transmissions. With luck, a skilled worker could produce twenty usable crystals a day. The United States Army's 1939 decision to convert its radio equipment to crystals resulted in a run on quartz, which in those days came primarily from Brazil. German U-boats might sink ships carrying quartz, and so the army took to flying the crystals home, so necessary were they to the war. Efforts to locate domestic sources of suitable quartz led geologists to Arkansas, California, western North Carolina, and southwestern Virginia. Almost all Virginia's crystals occurred, not in veins, but in the weathered soil. Many were turned in by farmers. Following World War II, researchers turned to manmade piezo ceramics, which were both more easily obtained and of surer quality than natural quartz. So that Virginia's crystals are no longer crucial to national security.

Though they are to my personal security, transporting me back to days when my children were young enough to think hunting such things on a mountain's flank a great way to spend an afternoon. More sacred than the jar of stones gathering dust in my basement are these memories, rock hard and crystal clear despite the years, enduring even as time wears me down.

THE SHENANDOAH SEA

When temperature inversions trap warm air in the valley, fog forms, islanding House, Jump, and Hogback Mountains, until noon, when the sun burns off the clouds, and the valley returns to being a valley. But while the fog lasts and I'm perched on a hill lapping House Mountain's flanks and I look over the southwest-trending archipelago of Short Hills, I believe in Thomas Jefferson's Shenandoah Sea, a mythic ocean that stretched from Blacksburg, Virginia, into Pennsylvania where it poured into the Atlantic with the Susquehanna River. Twenty miles wide, two thousand feet deep, three hundred miles long, the Shenandoah Sea was close cousin to those will-o'-the-wisp oceans sought by Europeans in search of the Northwest Passage, always just over the next hill, around the river's bend, over there, someplace else.

In *Notes on the State of Virginia*, Jefferson described Harpers Ferry as "one of the most stupendous scenes in nature . . . worth a voyage across the Atlantic," imagining it the relic of "a war between rivers and mountains." Dammed up by the Blue Ridge Mountains, the Potomac and Shenandoah rivers "formed an ocean which filled the whole valley; that continuing to rise they have at length broken over at this spot, and have torn the mountain down from its summit to its base. The piles of rock on each hand, but particularly on the Shenandoah, the evident marks of their disrupture and avulsion from their beds by the most powerful agents of nature, corroborate the impression." Charles Thomson corroborated his friend Jefferson's surmise, asserting that "what is now a fruitful vale was formerly a great lake or collection of water, which possibly might have here formed a mighty cascade, or had its vent to the ocean by the Susquehanna, where the Blue ridge seems to terminate." Thomson imagines it a southern version of the Great Lakes, and then wonders if the Gulf of Mexico itself might not have been "a champaign country," "a vast plain" flooded by the Atlantic's having breached "a continued range of mountains through Cuba, Hispaniola, Porto rico, Martinique, Guadaloupe, Barbados, and Trinidad." Salt or fresh, lake or ocean, the Shenandoah Valley was once water.

And fossil shells confirm the story. House Mountain's flanks rise from the valley floor as round and steep as a sleeping Leviathan's, and a scramble up one of

them leaves my son, Edward, and me sweating, a quick lick of the upper lip suggesting that the breeze cooling us as we sit under the tropic-shaped shade of an
ailanthus tree blows from off seas just over the hill. Shells litter the stone littoral
we sit on, the Confederate-gray lime matrix chockablock with the star-shaped
stalks of crinoids scattered like a fallen Milky Way among clamlike brachiopods
in beds as thick as mussels, the broken bowls of coral-like bryozoans, and, find of
finds, the three-lobed head of an occasional trilobite. At home, bookshelves heavy
with our trawl prove to even the most skeptical that what is land was once upon
a time water fathoms deep.

Jefferson and Thomson imagined Harpers Ferry a spectral Niagara Falls, the
Potomac and Shenandoah riverbeds still choked with remnants of the falls. The
Shenandoah Sea had just vanished, its vacant bed half moist, and if we but
squint when standing at Harpers Ferry we can almost see it lapping the sides of
the Blue Ridge and Allegheny mountains. Not so, says modern science, which has
not only pushed the sea back, back, back into the mists of time, but come at last
to deny its ever having existed.

Jefferson supposed, "The first glance of this scene hurries our senses into the
opinion, that this earth has been created in time, that the mountains were formed
first, that the rivers began to flow afterwards, that in this place particularly they
have been damned up by the Blue ridge of mountains.... " The devout of his time
thought otherwise, believing with Genesis that God had created the universe
in seven days, not "in time." Opinion divided on when the mountains had been
formed, some supposing them to have risen with Eden, others that they were the
remnants of Noah's Flood, carved out as the waters of the Deluge poured first
forth and then back into the fountains of the earth from whence they came. Modern science too is skeptical; Jefferson, though right in thinking "that this earth
has been created in time," got it backwards; the sea was first, the mountains and
rivers second.

In truth, there never was a Shenandoah Sea; the valley has long been just that,
a valley, dry land. The Shenandoah and Potomac rivers arose, it is thought, when
the mountains rose, gravity forcing the rising land to drain into rivers that ran
parallel to the resistant rocks of the Blue Ridge until they found a way eastward,
not in a cataclysmic Niagara Falls of a flood, but in a gentle and ever so gradual
erosion that still goes on today. And the rivers began, not six thousand years ago
as Genesis supposes, but 280 million years ago, when the drifting continents of
Africa and Europe and North America collided and formed a mountain range
perhaps as grand as the Alps that time and water have gradually worn away to
today's stumps. The continents backed away from each other, the Atlantic Ocean

widening at the glacially slow rate that fingernails grow, so that it took 220 million years to reach its current width.

The valley itself was once mountain, rising no one knows for sure how high, its billion of tons of rock dissolved and eroded eastward to the coastal plain, which is but sand from the vanished peaks of the Shenandoah Mountains. You can see this if you look at the flanks of the mountains enclosing today's Shenandoah Valley; the bedrock slants up, pointing skyward over the valley itself toward vanished mountaintops, back to a time when the mountains were laid low and the valleys exalted.

If ever there was a sea here, it was before all this, so way back that I have to imagine the years as quarters of inches laid out end to end on the earth, time a colossal ruler running westward from where I stand at the corner of Main and Nelson streets in Lexington. Columbus discovered America 128 inches ago, more than ten feet to the west; the Indians came across from Asia 2,500 inches ago, 208 feet west of here and 83 feet west of where Genesis has God creating the earth in 4000 B.C.E. Now the math gets tough. The dinosaurs died out 16,250,000 inches ago, 256 miles west of here, somewhere in West Virginia. The Atlantic Ocean began to spread 220 millions years ago—864 miles west of me, in Topeka, Kansas. The Blue Ridge and Allegheny began to rise 280 million years ago—1,104 miles west of here, near Dodge City, Kansas. And the valley's sea shells were laid down 400 million years ago in the Silurian period—1,600 miles west of here on my ruler, somewhere in Utah.

It's hard to get a handle on all this, especially when the view says otherwise. Taking the guide and survey books, I slowly, ever so slowly, decipher their geological jargon of allochthon, facies, graben, karst, anticline, scarp, slump, strata, strike-slip, and syncline so that the self-evident sea of the Shenandoah evaporates and the mythical mountains of Pangaea and its dissolution rise before me. For I am a believer. And what it is, in my case at least, is belief, not knowledge, which I came to understand when discussing a fossil rock embedded in the cafeteria wall of the college where I teach. Casually stating that the shells we saw were from the Silurian period, some four hundred million years old, I was caught short by a student who insisted that the earth was only six thousand years old and these shells the remains of Noah's Flood. And there we were: a born-again eighteen- year-old facing a middle-aged English teacher and what he half understood of modern geological theory. We still stand there, because, to be honest, I have no way of proving my beliefs any more than did the student. Thanks to his beliefs, however, I've read a half dozen books on the young-earth theorizers, Christians all, who take the Bible as their guide and fit the facts to its procrustean bed. And if I had not been inoculated by just whom I'm not sure—although high-school science teachers, television, and a certain predilection I have for following the crowd and toeing the line are good candidates—I could believe as well. The cataclysmic crowd who suppose these mountains remnants of a mighty flood of some kind, be it Noah's or the draining of the Shenandoah Sea, have appearances on their side, as the view confirms.

Even those who prefer a scientific explanation of the mountains around Lexington may mistake their origin. I've made a habit of asking Lexingtonians where they think House Mountain came from: volcanoes, the Ice Age, and plate tectonics are the most popular candidates. Just what the latter means no one seems sure, but they've all seen pictures of Pangaea in books and are believers. The Ice Agers are similar in their beliefs; they know there was an Ice Age in North America and incorrectly suppose it came through Virginia, carving out mountains as it went. The vulcanists, mistaken though they too be, have appearances on their side; House Mountain does look something like a truncated volcano when viewed from town. But were they to circumnavigate the mountain, they'd see the volcano transform itself into two breasts outside Collierstown and a narrow defile in Denmark.

Lexington's share of the Great Valley seems all too tranquil a setting for plate tectonics. To believe in them, I have to drive west to North Mountain, where John Jordan's old toll road to glory snakes its scary way seven miles up and seven miles down. Here the sandstone ridge cap slants at a near 45 degree angle so that you have to clamber up its fissured and cracked surface to perch at the edge of nothing and look out at House Mountain seemingly within spitting distance and begin to understand that something humongous sat down somewhere to so push these rocks out of their original horizontal alignment. It's tempting to think that the something sat somewhere behind you to the west, since the rock sinks down that way, but the ones who know say that these west-sinking sandstones are part of a huge section of eastern Virginia crumpled up and pushed so far west by the wandering continent of Africa that the rock formations visible in the valley repeat themselves underground, as if a massive stack of rugs had folded upon itself. North Mountain's two-thousand-foot rise from the valley floor represents merely the ragged remnants of long worn-away layers of this carpet.

What caps these mountains may slant today, but the geologists say it was laid down as sandy beach and shoal 425 million years ago in a Silurian-aged Cape Hatteras flanking mountains somewhere to the east, where today there is only the Piedmont, the Atlantic coastal plain, and the Atlantic Ocean, the mountains having eroded away long, long ago. Jefferson was right in a way. The Shenandoah

Sea did exist, though long before the Shenandoah Valley was carved from the mountains we see today. And it stretched, the savants say, west into today's Great Plains.

The view alone is worth the drive up one of our mountains some morning when the fog hangs low in the valley and Jefferson's sea is wholly believable and to sit and watch the clouds dissolve and science's reasonable if less-than-exciting view of landscape prevail again. Then you know that whatever cataclysm, rapid or slow, carved out this valley had aesthetics on its side. And you will look and see, like God, that it is good.

CAVES

Many a valley resident has reason enough to lament that we live in karst country. Unlike our usual two-dimensional perception of topography, karst topography, named after Kras, a region in Slovenia, exists in three dimensions, often reaching invisibly hundreds of feet underground. So in Rockbridge County what you see may not be what you get. My friend Celia built a pond whose depth fluctuates wildly as its accumulated waters—each pint pressing its pound of weight earthward—push their way out through invisible subterranean channels. I had a well drilled three hundred feet beneath the local Maury River's level and could have descended farther in search of water that, one might erroneously believe, would sink no lower than the local river. The Shenandoah Valley's limestone is like a giant block of Swiss cheese, riddled with holes that lead hither and yon, carved through the millennia by acid rain's dissolution of carbonate bedrock. And though I cannot locate the caves that seduce Celia's waters from their beds, I have followed waters underground into the marvel that is the caves of Rockbridge County.

My favorite cave lies along Cold Run, which enters the Maury near Whistle Creek. Running underneath Charlie Showalter's cedar-crowded hills, this cave has been carved by a still extant creek, too small to have garnered a name, but which has been, judging from the size of the cave it has carved, dissolving rock for many thousand years. Low, dark, and narrow, the entry of the cave is easily missed, hidden as it is by the low-hanging boughs of sycamore and cedar that line Cold Run's banks. But, known, there it is, an open-sesame miracle emerging from the hill's cloven side of solid rock, a four- by six-foot source of cool air and darkness that invites even the most cautious of explorers on a hot summer's day.

So it was that, twenty years ago, I foolhardily stooped and entered the cave with but a flashlight for company. The baby creek responsible for the marvel I had entered seems scarcely capable of having carved its way through the half mile of solid rock that it has; nor does there seem, from outside, room for the cavern, which reaches skyward a hundred feet through what was once solid Virginia bedrock but which is now an airy nothingness capped with a dome of rock that, when I am standing under it, appears both ponderous and tenuous. I have to

A valley cave. From Henry Howe, *Historical Collections of Virginia* (Charleston, S.C.: William R. Babcock, 1845)

bend over the first twenty feet or so, following the creek's narrow channel through blue gray limestone, the creek's bottom a series of ripples carved in bedrock, until the cave opens up and the roof rises twenty, thirty, fifty, one hundred feet above me and the first of the stalactites drips downward. The creek bends and snakes its way as deviously through solid rock as its cousins do through open air, and, several ox bows in, I pass through an erotic passage lined with clay red udders of swollen rock begging to be stroked, in whose crevices sleep bats no longer than my shortest finger. The creek itself swirls coolly around my tennis-shoe-clad feet, and when I stop, the steady drip drip drip of water is all I hear. Switch off the flashlight and profound darkness descends.

Even farther in I hear the unclear babble of what seem voices; these gradually resolve into the sound of running water that finally materializes as an underground waterfall, flanked by flowstones that sparkle in the flashlight's beam and seem, now brain corals, and now terraced rice paddies. Every now and then I have to crawl through passages narrow enough to fool me into thinking I'm trapped, but which release me with a scrape and a twist, or under a rockfall that blocks the narrow defile and makes me look toward the distant roof with apprehension. I then realize the broken slabs are covered with a melted icing of mineral deposits thousands of years in the making, which causes me to pause yet again when I reflect that the deposits had to have come from the ceiling, which erodes more and more each year until it becomes a fragile fretwork of rock waiting to crush whoever's fool enough to walk beneath it. I walk, crawl, and scramble to what seems the end of the cavern, where the roof slopes down toward the floor and I'm on all fours looking at a shallow stream of water that flows out from where the ceiling meets the floor. I then realize that the floor is mud and that if I prostrate myself and inch along ever so slowly through the mud I can swim farther under the cavern roof. Holding my nose barely above the water and careful not to bang my head on the ceiling, I make my way twenty feet through a mud bath to another cave beyond, one that opens up on a jumble of rocks still jagged from their fall to earth. I scramble round and over and under and finally see light and clamber up, up, up through a narrow cleft to the outside world, which is still, miraculously, there, wider and brighter and realer than it seemed an hour ago when I entered the underworld. I find myself in a sinkhole recent enough to still be filled at the bottom with a jumble of rock through which the creek that cut it sneaks. Those who know such things tell me that many of Rockbridge County's sinkholes date to the end of the last Ice Age, when falling water tables led the caves of subterranean streams to pock the land with their collapse. But ten thousand years of fill have smoothed these holes and hidden the telltale jumble of rocks that betray the one time presence of a cave, so that this ragged, rock-filled crater may well be younger.

A straight shot through a hillside, with no hidden crevices and no need of ropes or serious climbing, my cave is safe enough to venture in alone, or to take into it groups of children eager to explore a "wild" cave, so that a yearly expedition has become a birthday tradition, we traipsing through the cow-filled pastures to the creekside, little boys scanning the banks in order to be the first to discover the entry into another world, and we all becoming covered with mud and bruises as we bang and crawl and climb and swim our way through terra incognita, emerging hours later laden with mud and memories.

The Greeks believed that the river Styx emerged in a small stream in Arcadia and that Acheron flowed into Lake Acherousia, which is now rice fields. But my unnamed stream through the underworld shelters only temporary refugees from life's sunlit regions: pack rats whose smelly leaf and stick mounds litter ledges and tunnels near the entrance; bats that cling silently through the winter on rock walls deep enough to stay at a constant fifty-five degrees; spiders foraging for wayward flies in the dark; and crayfish clambering through the muddy, rock-strewn floor of the stream. Because the stream is subterranean for only a short distance, its waters are constantly refreshed from outside, and floods sometimes scour the cave, none of its denizens is adapted to life without sunlight.

But there are two such animals in Rockbridge County, an amphipod and a planarian, which are now permanent occupants of Hades. Like their remote ancestors, who long ago crawled down a hole and never returned, I know the ambiguous attraction of such portals into other realms, those deep romantic chasms that slant down green hills athwart their cedarn covers, that Orpheus, Ulysses, and Dante clambered through: to leave this world for another, a realm as near as the holes beneath our feet, yet so remote we often remain oblivious to its proximity until a road collapses or a house sags. We learn that this solid earth we walk upon is rotten with holes, as precarious as a child's block tower, and that what seems sure and certain is an illusion, that there are depths beneath us as profound as those within us, that the darkness within finds its literal expression below, and that, who knows, all this we call reality is but a wafer-thin veneer waiting to fall into what lies beneath.

ROCK CASTLES

Little House Mountain, the closer ridge to Lexington, hides a castle on its summit. Where it rises highest, the sandstone bedrock has eroded into a warren of room-sized mini mesas, each rising twenty feet above the ground, separated from its neighbors by narrow, winding corridors perfect for getting lost in, playing hide and seek, and imagining yourself lord or lady of a castle. The mesas themselves are flat, largely bare rock, inviting campsites with magnificent views. The sandstones that cap House Mountain and a number of other area ridges were laid down 450 million years ago, when this area was the continental edge; pick up a handful of their component sands from atop your mountain perch and feel grains that have not been loose since the first land plants were emerging from the sea. These were Silurian times; the geologists think that the sandy beaches built up as the ancestor to today's Atlantic, the Iapetus Ocean, closed and, closing, pushed up mountains that, eroding, poured their sands seaward in sandbanks as massive as those off today's Hatteras. The easiest place locally to find these sandstones is Goshen Pass, where the Maury has cut a dramatic seven-mile-long gorge a football field wide, and, quadrangle guide in hand, you can trace their track along the narrow roadbed that snakes between the river and the six-hundred-foot-high walls of nearly vertical rock. Here the sandstone has been folded over onto itself, and you see the same strata again and again and again.

The stone on House Mountain is much less thick. You can see this cap especially well in winter from Lexington, its near vertical form easily identifiable from afar. Beneath this sandstone cap lies a much thicker layer of limestone and shale buried under the rubble of collapsing sandstone but sufficiently resistant to provide a less precipitous angle of repose for the lower levels of House Mountain. A glance at any topo map of the mountain reveals a similar picture; regularly paced contour lines grow illegibly close as you approach the top of House, a visual indication of increasing verticality and almost all limited to the sandstone cap.

The mountain is remarkably small on the state's geological and topographical maps. You'd think a landmark as massive and important as House Mountain would maintain its importance on a map, but no, it nearly disappears when looked at cartographically, and its summit, which dominates the western skyline of Lexington, is but two thumbprint-sized daubs of purple paint nearly lost in a sea of washed-out pink. The pink is the agreed-upon color for the Martinsburg Formation, a fossil-rich skirt of limestone and shale that defines House Mountain's lower slopes. The purple daubs, one dark, one lighter, are geologists' shades for the mountain's sandstone summit. Shale is structurally weak, and the Martinsburg Formation is, everywhere in Rockbridge County, folded upon itself in multiple repeating layers and cleaved into a thousand thousand incomprehensible fragments, which, when exposed, are filled with fossils. These detritus-free slopes are hard to find, and rockhounds are loathe to tell their secret sites. I will but say that here and there upon the mountain's lower slopes are fields of fossils, stones filled haphazardly with the remains of animals that perished four hundred million years ago, before the dinosaurs, before the reptiles, before land animals or plants, back when trilobites were king. I have found trilobites as small as my little finger, as large as my hand, some entire but most fragmentary, their lobed heads and segmented abdomens littering the rock in places I have divulged only to family. Accompanying them are fragmentary crinoids, sedentary starfish impaled upon star-shaped trunks, so that a bit of seabed seems a petrified fragment of the Milky Way thrown to earth for my delight. Brachiopods are the most commonly preserved residents of these muds, their shell-like head gear resembling a clam closed in upon itself or, if presented in profile, a comma etched against a gray background, palm-sized fragments of long dead reefs making paper weights excellent for dreaming on when trapped at work.

If I climb higher than these fossils, struggling up from the well-watered hardwood valleys to the drier piney ridges that reach summitward like arthritic fingers—a vegetable succession traceable from Lexington, where the evergreen pine ridges stand out year around against spring green, fall yellow, and gray winter valleys—I eventually reach the first ramparts of sandstone, ten-foot walls that make what I have been scrambling up seem child's play. This is thick-bedded, whitish quartzite, hard, nearly free of impurities, pure quartz found throughout the Appalachians from New York to Tennessee, and the crown jewel of nearly every ridge in the Great Valley of Virginia. While I could scratch the crumbly Martinsburg shales with my fingernail, this sandstone—known variously as Tuscarora, Clinch, or Massanutten sandstone thanks to its independent description by different geologists during the nineteenth century—is so hard and fine it breaks my fingernail. Set back and above it like a layer on a wedding cake is another sandstone, thicker and sometimes difficult to distinguish from the Tuscarora. But this, the Clinton Formation sandstone, often begins as thin beds of iron-rich, red sandstone, as it does in places where it is exposed on Little House Mountain. Easily recognizable, this blood-colored stone, lying in broken slabs on the mountain tops, erodes into rounded cobbles as it slides down the mountain flanks. Many a valley field has one or more rock piles, which two centuries of farmers laboriously made by clearing their fields of cobbles, and here and there along the cliffs of the Maury are cobbly patches of ground that mark the bed of an ancient creek whose descendant often as not flows upstream or downstream today. These cobbles are mostly white and yellow fragments of harder sandstones, but a good minority are rounded red fragments of House Mountain itself. Inscribed upon these mountain slabs are trace fossils, crisscrossing bas-relief squiggles of what were once underwater worm tunnels.

Above these platelike slabs of reddish rock rises the castle proper, thick-bedded, gray sandstone walls, often as smooth as mortuary rock. Geologists claim that the chambers and hallways of the castle are but wider versions of the narrow fissures fracturing today's walls, crevices into which water crept and froze and thawed and froze and thawed, expanding and cracking and slowly dissolving the sandstone Ice Age after Ice Age. The valley castles are remnants of that frozen era, when the top of House Mountain was little more than tundra and when ice waged a winning battle against rock on these heights, cracking and leveraging the rock mesas over the edge to tumble valleyward. Student Rock on Little House's summit is one of these cantilevered disasters, a house-sized rock monster you can scramble up and out on to view Lexington from a perch as slanting as a roof. Caught in mid-fall, Student Rock waits for another Ice Age to complete its tumble, while similar rocks lie hidden in the trees below, scattered like blocks in giants' play. There is a calculus to their size, for down below where humans live, the rocks are rarely car sized, and by the time they get to Lexington, having traveled there via Whistle Creek and the Maury River, they are river jacks, concrete-block-sized rocks just right for building walls. Elsewhere beneath the ramparts of the castle are talus slopes of smaller, table-sized rocks, jumbled and tumbled together in a frozen rock cascade. You can see similar talus slopes on the sides of mountains as you drive Interstate 81 up and down the valley, gray rock flows fanning out downslope, marking where erosion was most active in the Ice Age gone these ten thousand years. Treeless and tempting though they are to climb as shortcuts to the top, these are treacherous staircases. Although they haven't moved in thousands of years, as the nearly solid crust of lichens testifies, they are but precariously piled one on top of the other and liable to tip over under a climber's weight. Or to harbor rattlers in their dark depths; it was in just such a rock jumble that they found the "largest rattlesnake in the South," which you can still see in the fireworks stand out on Lee Highway.

Each castle is unique, having eroded in its own way. North Mountain's castle surprises you. One minute you're on a narrow ridge trail, the next you're on broad ramparts, the castle hanging to the mountain's western face, its surface a chess board whose squares are separated by narrow chasms twenty feet deep. Forge Mountain's unexpected marvel hides in a forest whose trunks are as gray as the grainy stones piled as tight as those in the Peruvian city of Cuzco, and through whose breaches the trail tumbles.

And one remembers House Mountain for its claustrophobic corridors whose hollow rings hint at hidden dungeons. One day Edward had me bushwhack him and his dog up, up, up House Mountain's vertiginous face to "his" castle, only to discover, after two hours of my carrying boy and dog, that what he remembered as House was, actually, North Mountain. No matter; what's important is that a rock castle so captured his imagination that he'd take his dog and dad to see it, even if it was the wrong castle. And one day, he'll climb with his child to a castle that haunts his memory.

Atop House Mountain's mini mesas, you feel you're on solid bedrock, that it is all Virginia rock straight down to wherever China begins in the insides of the earth and that you are safe and secure and emperor of all that you can see—which is quite a lot on a good day. Off to the east the Blue Ridge runs along the horizon, while between you and it the Great Valley of Virginia opens itself to your gaze, House Mountain's forests giving way to a patchwork of forested hill and open field rolling down to the Maury and back up to the Blue Ridge.

To the west lies Big House, its trees seemingly almost touchable, and around its western tip North Mountain and the Alleghenies, ridge after ridge of mountain fading into the blue breath of a million trees. Almost flat, the mesa tops are fissured by narrow cracks in which sand and seed and root have caught and a crew of herbs and trees eke out existence here.

Huckleberries are plentiful, loving as they do the acidic, nearly pure sand soil up here. I have lunched on them in the fall, beating the mice and birds to them, and nibbled the less plentiful wintergreen's grainy red berries, which taste just like their namesake gum. Table Mountain pines struggle in this rock to reach five feet in height. Tortured by wind and ice, these rugged trees are endemic to the Appalachians, growing only here, in a narrow band on the dry, inaccessible upper ridges where they serve no human purpose other than beauty, but do that admirably, perched as they are on see-forever, precipitous mountain ledges, their branches bonsaied by prevailing winds, their trunks the only back support this near the edge of nothing.

I've camped upon these summits, fondly supposing myself for a night the nearest to heaven of valley residents, caught midway between the Milky Way and Lexington's earthly galaxy of streetlights half hid by Brushy Hill. Such elevated ruminations fall as the moon rises over the dark line of the Blue Ridge, and memories colder than stone seep in, lost loves and dead friends walking my private Elsinore, accusing me of being me. Then Japanese poet Doï Bansui asks yet again, "Now the castle ruin's nightfallen moon / Unchanging light, for whom might it be? / Remaining on the hedge are only vines, / Singing on the pine only the winds."

⚘ THE NATURAL BRIDGE

The Natural Bridge of Virginia so awed Thomas Jefferson that he wrote, "Few men have resolution to walk to [it] and look over into the abyss. You involuntarily fall on your hands and feet, creep to the parapet and peep over it. Looking down from this height about a minute, gave me a violent head ach [*sic*]." You can no longer share this headache, today's owners having erected a wooden fence on each side of U.S. Highway 11 as it crosses the arch so that you can no longer look down. Gone are the days of unsuspecting passengers crying to David Hunter Strother (pen name: Porte Crayon) in dismay, "How could you do it! The bridge! the bridge! we're on the bridge!" or when Chateaubriand's René might bury his beloved Atala in Groves of Death guarded by "a wonderful creation—a natural bridge, like the one in Virginia, of which you may have heard" or when Melville wrote of Moby Dick that "for an instant his whole marbleized body formed a high arch, like Virginia's Natural Bridge, and warningly waving his bannered flukes in the air, the grand god revealed himself, sounded, and went out of sight" or when French wallpaper featured the bridge in conjunction with Niagara Falls. Gone even are the days when waggish Washington and Lee students convinced the gullible that the bridge itself had burned down.

And yet the bridge stunned me my first visit, though I had to content myself with viewing it from below, where, Jefferson assures us, "It is impossible for the emotions arising from the sublime, to be felt beyond what they are here: so beautiful an arch, so elevated, so light, and springing as it were up to heaven, the rapture of the spectator is really indescribable!" Perhaps, perhaps; but one detects a bit of the travel agent in Jefferson's *Notes on the State of Virginia*, and whether the bridge is, as he would have it, "the most sublime of Nature's works" is debatable, at least to someone not a native son. Still, with the all-too-heavy span of rock—ninety feet long and wide, forty-five feet thick—two hundred feet above you, and trucks traversing that, you have only two seconds should it fall, as fragments have, so fulfilling Edmund Burke's musings that "the passion caused by the great and sublime in nature . . . is Astonishment; and astonishment is that state of the soul, in which all its motions are suspended, with some degree of horror." In this case, it is the horror of being squashed by falling rock.

Natural Bridge of Virginia. From Henry Howe, *Historical Collections of Virginia* (Charleston, S.C.: William R. Babcock, 1845)

For fallen it has, from revolutionary cataclysm to slow, almost boring erosion. Jefferson described the bridge as "on the ascent of a hill, which seems to have been cloven through its length by some great convulsion," no doubt the same he thought had created the passage at Harpers Ferry, both it and the Natural Bridge "monuments of a war between rivers and mountains, which must have shaken the earth itself to its center." At the Natural Bridge, Jefferson thought, "The two sides had parted asunder . . . [a] portion in that instance having held together, during the separation of the other parts, so as to form a bridge over the Abyss." That separation, that war which shook the earth to its center, was to Jefferson a natural equivalent to the shot heard round the world, the political revolution he participated in. Not so, sober-sided science interjected as early as 1818, when Francis William Gilmer proclaimed that, rather than the bridge's "being the effect of a sudden convulsion, or an extraordinary deviation from the ordinary laws of nature, it will be found to have been produced by the slow operation of causes which have always, and must ever continue, to act in the same manner." Rather than revolution, we too now believe in erosion, slow but so steady; yes, even the paltry Cedar Creek flowing under the bridge could have, given time enough, worn away the hill of which the bridge is but a minor rib. It is an ancient, Paleozoic rib, composed of limestone and dolomite deposited during the Ordovician period 450 million years ago, uplifted and deformed over the ages, and worn, down, down, down over the last 200 million years—time enough to cut a cave, collapse a cave, and leave a bridge. Erosion is a fitting metaphor for those who feel we live in lesser days.

If science happily lessened nature's awe and stretched time out until it vanished, religion refused to. The bridge has long attracted those drawn to finding God through nature. The Monacan Indians say that the Great Spirit miraculously created the bridge to allow them to escape from their enemies and were also the first to find the bridge proof of a God who works in time and on nature. Nineteenth-century folk artist Edward Hicks reinvented the bridge as the pathway from this world to the spiritual paradise Isaiah promised, when "the wolf also shall dwell with the lamb, and the leopard shall lie down with the kid; and the calf and the young lion and the fatling together; and a little child shall lead them," America holding promise as a—perhaps the—New World. Less prophetic than profitable, the Drama of Creation has been retold nightly on the walls of the bridge, since 1927, when President Calvin Coolidge first illuminated it. And, free of charge, local Christians still celebrate Easter sunrise service at the bridge.

Naturally Edward and I trekked there. We paid to see the bridge, which, unlike so many of America's natural wonders, is private and has been since Jefferson himself bought it in 1754. We paid to see as well the Natural Bridge Caverns, the Natural Bridge Wax Museum, the Natural Bridge Toy Museum, Professor Cline's Haunted Monster Museum, Professor Cline's Dino Kingdom, and Professor Cline's Foamhenge. Of all these wonders, natural and unnatural, what least impressed my son was the Natural Bridge. How could a mere Bridge "higher than Niagara, older than the dawn" compete with what the *Washington Post* called "One of the Seven Weird Wonders of Virginia," where "Scooby Doo meets the Twilight Zone"?

Huckstering natural wonders is a fine American tradition. Who knows how much wampum the canny Monacans made off their obvious in with the Almighty? And even Jefferson built a cabin with a guest room at the Natural Bridge. By 1828 the bridge boasted its own hotel and enjoyed a flurry of popularity as a natural wonder. Following the Civil War, however, visitors waned, if sporadic articles in the *New York Times* are accurate. One writer observed in 1869 that "Of late years it has languished in obscurity and neglect," and another, exposing the 1873 burning of the bridge, sneered that "Bridges are not and cannot be made popular, and the public taste, which just now sets strongly in the direction of the hot springs and canyons of the Yellowstone, will not be attracted to the Natural Bridge by any quantity of blazing tar and fainting colored persons." Even sympathetic visitors tended to patronize the bridge's purported sublimity; Porte Crayon related how he himself dared not imitate a daring damsel who'd perched on a stump at the edge of the precipice, and he supposed the rock outline on the arch's underside of the American Eagle vanquishing the British Lion—which must have predated the Revolution—to have been prophetic.

Not that adjacent attractions detract. As one Web site promoting private ownership of natural wonders explains, "Anyone looking for tacky signs of crass commercialism will not find them there. The property's owner has seen to it that the public can view the site's natural splendor in a manner that in no way detracts from its pristine beauty." Just be sure, you close your eyes until you get within the site. With such a god's plenty nearby, who can but marvel, with Jefferson, that "in the neighbourhood of the natural bridge, are people who have passed their lives within half a dozen miles, and have never been to survey these monuments"?

STONE WALLS

The walls of House Mountain sink slowly back into the earth from which they were raised with few to mourn their collapse. Two hundred years ago the hardscrabble House Mountain men raised these monuments to muscle by clearing their fields. Today those who climb House Mountain and its county kin, North Mountain and the Blue Ridge, come upon these memorials to a vanished people. These men were the first to carve farms out of the forests that clung to the mountain's sides, clearing fields up the nearly vertical higher slopes of both tree and rock; they chopped the former down to build their cabins, whose rock-lined root cellars and occasional half-tumbled-down chimneys still remember these homesteaders' dreams, and they lugged the latter to their fields' edges to build walls that bounded their tenuous claims to the land. Sometimes today's road up the mountain follows the walls, whose foundations now sit on ground as much as a foot higher than the roadbed, testifying to the ongoing erosion of House Mountain. At other times, the walls go off through the forest on their own, marking fields and boundaries whose purposes vanished with their proprietors generations ago.

Hidden in the forests that have reclaimed these mountains, these walls are a grander work than many might suppose. Over on the Blue Ridge is a still-standing, seven-mile-long wall built by mountain men herding their cattle in what were summer pastures but are now mostly woods. The forest service generously brush hogs Cole Mountain's top so that hikers can imagine what the world of these mountain herders must have been like. And from Cole Mountain you can see a Pisgah's worth of valley and piedmont splayed out before you and know yourself free of the worrisome world of littler people thousands of feet beneath you.

What calculus of rock and time dictates that this section of a wall stand and that decay? Anyone who spends a day or two alone building a wall with fieldstones rediscovers what fence builders through the ages have rediscovered or had passed on to them. Place the larger stones on the bottom; if possible, build a double row and have the stones slant inward so that the weight of stones above anchors stones below. Build like brick masons do: two on one and one on two, tying two stones' jointure together with one laid over top, no jointure touching another. Fill in the middle with lesser rocks, and cap the whole thing off with larger, flat stones that tie the sides together.

Such capstones are rare on House Mountain, where the stones are mainly concrete block size and often rounded off from tumbling downhill, so that the walls often lack anything tying them together other than their own inward-slanted weight. This has been insufficient over the years to keep them upright. Thigh-high and often only two- or three-courses tall, the stones cannot fall far, and a wall, though collapsed, will still delineate a boundary, though not as crisply as it did four generations ago.

But not all walls fall, and that standing where House Mountain residents say a mountain church once stood remains for the most part upright, having been built especially large and long lasting. Huge boulders, five feet by five, make up a part of it and must have been manhandled into place by several men and perhaps a horse or ox or two. This was no solitary farmer spending his less hectic hours clearing his field but a group effort to erect a wall to the greater glory of God and the community. And it has lasted longer than the church, which has vanished without a trace, and longer than the nearby graveyard, whose inhabitants, too poor to afford the marble markers of valley cemeteries, contented themselves with fieldstones that today look no different from those scattered by nature's random hand throughout these woods.

Those larger rocks upon which these religious men "builded their wall" proved too heavy for Jack Frost to heave. For he is the "something there is that doesn't love a wall." Every winter he freezes the ground and rocks, and after every freeze and thaw the rock wall gives an ever-so-slight shaking of its shoulders, a wouldn't-notice shiver that eventually tumbles stones. Frost heave grows rocks in newly cleared fields, the frost actually lifting the rocks bit by bit through the soil, which settles in the spaces under rocks, thereby moving them miraculously up through the soil where they sprout like mushrooms every spring to the weary annoyance of farmers. New England fields were famous for their yearly rock crops, which provided material for the miles of rock walls there. House Mountain's slopes superficially resemble New England's glacial till, both being a jumble of sand and rocks of varying sizes, originally held in place by forest cover that kept the frost from sinking too deep into the soil. When the trees fell and the leaf litter blew away, nothing protected the now bare soil, and the frosts reached deeper, heaving up rock after rock, which the farmers in turn heaved into the walls that now tumble back into the ground from which they came. But the larger rocks that took several men to heave into place ignore the feeble nudges of frost, sitting solidly where they were placed as foundation stones, their sections of wall still standing where they were laid two hundred years ago.

The House Mountain men had more in common with New England than walls; they were ardent Unionists. Their small, mountainous holdings had no use for slavery or for slavers who hid behind the high sounding sentiment of states rights. And just before the Civil War, they nearly came to blows with secessionists at the Virginia Military Institute. After one incipient riot when VMI cadets marched with their rifles downtown looking for a group of House Mountain men falsely accused of having killed some cadets, then professor of artillery Thomas Jackson—later nicknamed Stonewall—famously opined of war that one should, "draw the sword and throw away the scabbard." Jackson and many cadets died in the war they longed for, a war won by the House Mountain men. Not that you'd know it today in Lexington, where the memory of the Confederacy remains strong, and the 30 percent of Rockbridge County who were enslaved in 1860 have been forgotten by most of us.

But more than politics divided the mountain men from their valley neighbors. Walls are made of limestone in the valley and of sandstone on the mountains, thanks to the underlying geology. Limestone erodes more rapidly than sandstone, so shapely limestone walls in the valley are likely to contain a fair number of quarried stones. The fieldstones around Lexington are hardly shapely, having been tumbled about for eons in their slow roll toward the ocean. I know a valley house built of limestone whose road-fronting façade is composed of shaped and quarried stones, but whose less public sides and rear were laid with cheaper, rougher hewn field stones. Iron ore and canal magnate John Jordan's hilltop brick mansion overlooking the terminus of the Maury River canal is one of the few valley places still flanked with drystone walls made up of thousands of plate-sized limestone fragments whose placement must have been as tedious as it was effective. One or two houses in town are built from what, by their shape, must be field stones, but the majority of city walls and foundations are quarried lime, much of which contains fossils from when the stone was seabed four hundred and more million years ago. Clamlike brachiopods, lacey bryozoans, and fragments of crinoids litter the blue gray stone, which is often shot through with veins of bright white calcite deposited by calcium-rich water percolating through ancient fractures in the rock.

The valley is littered with forgotten quarries and rock walls and foundations. Every decent-sized stream had its mill, and moldering away beside many of them are the scattered stones that made up mill walls. When Edward and I trespass up

Whistle Creek, we come to one hidden in the brush. Steal a mile further upstream and we come to yet another. Canoeing the Maury above Lexington, we float beside Furr's six-foot-high mill race, a stone retaining wall capped today with box elder and sycamore on whose bedrock bottom we walk dry shod and hunt for trilobites, but which but two generations ago was filled with Maury water to power the mill, only recently bulldozed. To get an idea of what a valley mill was like, Edward and I have to drive north for fifteen miles to Wade's Mill, a working eighteenth-century flour mill whose water-driven millworks are a clattering wonder of slapping belts and turning cogs, all coated with a fine white powder of corn and wheat and buckwheat and rye, a bag or two of which we buy each time we visit to make our morning pancakes.

What fields near Lexington are not yet suburbs often contain piles of field-stones too small to use for building and heaped up years ago by farmers patiently clearing their fields. These piles contain a mix of lime and sandstone, the pre-dominant sandstones remnants of larger rocks that tumbled down from the mountains long ago, back when the Maury and its attendant creeks flowed through a landscape long since eroded. You can wade across the Maury River at Lexington today, where its bed is a jumble of river jacks, football-sized boulders washed downriver from Goshen Pass, where the river cuts through North Mountain, exposing bed after bed of multicolored sandstone. Geologists can heft a river cobble in Lexington and tell you what formation it came from in Goshen and then recount the story of eroding mountains and rising seas vanished for hundreds of millions of years. About all I know is that if you hold one of these boulders, you're holding the top of House Mountain in your hand. If you follow these fieldstones mountainward, they grow gradually larger, until you come to the feet of the mountains themselves.

Here at the foot of the mountain, builder-sized stones litter the ground. Cream colored, light brown, maroon, they break easily and straightly along frac-ture lines and make as pretty a stone wall as you might want. Philip Clayton, who lives where Sugar Creek begins its precipitous climb up House Mountain's south-east flank, has spent gallons of sweat and not a few bruises chipping the stones flung higgledy-piggledy across his fields and creek banks into rectangles he lays in walls and foundations. His walls are multicolored scraps of the mountain knit together with thin seams of mortar, maroon squares and cream and brown rec-tangles in a stony crazy quilt of beauty. Clayton builds for eternity, however, mortaring his walls. Farther up House Mountain, in the woods that begin on his property, are his predecessors' unmortared walls and foundations.

Wherever there is free-flowing water on House Mountain's slopes, you'll find a cabin site. Its snaggletoothed chimney may well be the first thing to catch your eye, rising grayly among a forest of sixty- to eighty-year-old trees. Reach that chimney and you'll find at its feet a depression in the ground, what remains of the cabin's root cellar, gradually filling in with detritus from the collapsed house and the yearly layer of leaves winter strews on this grave to frustrated dreams. Saddest of all perhaps are the remnant flowers of the woman of the cabin, a handful of daffodils blooming in spring at the foot of the chimney, a scattering of shade-stunted yuccas, and a carpet of periwinkle, all but the last succumbing to the ever thickening forest canopy. You can tell these were poor people this high up the mountain; only the desperate, driven from the valley's sweet calcium, would try farming such sandy, acidic soils. Even their chimneys bespeak their penury. In the valley, old chimneys are stone only partway up, brick having been used for the chimneys' upper lengths because it was lighter and easier to work with and allowed for larger flues. But all House Mountain's higher cabins boast chimneys of field stone all the way up, making them squatter and thicker and less costly in money though far more costly in time and effort than their rich valley cousins. Nor did lack of water deter at least one optimistic settler, whose well was dug through thirty feet of rocky jumble to where Whistle Creek's hidden headwaters trickle across bedrock. Its sides, barely wide enough for a man's shoulders to fit through, are lined with the rock through which its creator dug.

Of settlers' dreams, only the stones and flowers remain, the flowers fading and stones now as gray as the trunks of the trees growing up around them. Once they shared the colored glory of Philip Clayton's red and white and brown rock walls, but time and lichens and dirt have long since dimmed their palette, and they are as colorlessly gray as the leaves down into which they sink today, sad, straggling heaps of unhewn stones, all that is left of unknown settlers' fancies.

GEOLOGICAL SEGREGATION

Exasperated at his refusal to obey, I warned Edward, "If you don't behave, I'm gonna put you in the back of the bus," a threat which, happily, he didn't understand. Segregation's been gone for half a century, and if southerners my age remember when buses and nearly everything else were divided along racial lines, our children don't. Having swum through segregation until my teenage years with nary a thought about its perversity, I find Edward's indignation that "you actually let them do that to people" proof that dreams do come true. It is also testimony to my own depravity, since, at three in the morning when I'm not pretending to be a better person than I really am, I acknowledge, if only to my own accusing voices, that my break with segregation had more to do with teenage rejection of anything and everything my father stood for than the triumph of an inner moral compass.

So, unlike me, Edward is unaware that there are white and black cemeteries in town, white and black parts of town, that the upstairs mini theaters at the movie theater replace the black balcony of fifty years ago, that his middle school was once for blacks only. He's not the only one, either. I was talking to a new white colleague the other day, who, when I mentioned the black part of town, said, "You mean there're blacks in Lexington? I've never seen any." The remark was an exaggeration, I hope, though, for too many, Lexington's black community is nearly as invisible as Ralph Ellison's anonymous hero in *Invisible Man,* who lives in a basement "that was shut off and forgotten during the nineteenth century." It took us a little longer, but we've done such a fine job of whitewashing our black history that most people here think slavery a minor hiccup in a yeoman-filled valley, the very model of a whites-only Jeffersonian democracy. But the 1860 United States census tells a different story: of Rockbridge County's 17,248 residents, 4,407— nearly 25 percent—were black or mulatto, of whom 3,985 were slave. And nearly 30 percent—697—of Lexington's 2,135 residents were black or mulatto, of whom 606 were slaves. Today's Lexington is a pallid version of yesterday's two parallel worlds, one black, one white, gone with the winds of integration. Older residents remember black grocery stores, black clubs, black doctors, black barbers, black water fountains, black movie balconies, black waiting rooms, black funeral parlors, black cemeteries, black churches. Today, only the barber, church, and cemetery remain, all three reduced to taking whites.

If racism wrote the zoning laws segregating the races, geology determined where the races lived. Gilbert Campbell's ford over the Maury River meant Lexington, Virginia, so named in a paroxysm of patriotism in 1778, rose where it did, on the edge of a break in the river's sixty-foot high cliffs, alongside a road so steep that later generations shoveled dirt downslope to lessen the angle of descent, an engineering feat that left what had been ground-floor doors opening into vacant air, as some still do to this day. Once atop the cliffs, though, the land leveled out, and much of Lexington is laid out on nearly level lots. Not so Diamond Hill, Green Hill, and Mudtown, where blacks located on land so sinkhole-riddled that to this day lots are up and down things, Maury and Senseney streets roller coasters for wagon-riding children, and a hike up Diamond Street not for the faint of heart or out of shape. If Diamond and Green Hills earned their reputations by perching over sinkholes no self-respecting white man would build on, Mudtown earned its by occupying a sinkhole vast enough to plant a neighborhood in. Not that history isn't ironic. Some of the town's best views are those in Diamond Hill, looking west toward House and Jump and Hogback mountains. And those blacks who bought land long ago along the edge of the main east–west road through town now sit on prime business real estate, fast food and gas stations and grocery stores happy to rent or buy from them.

Money being money, blacks weren't the only people subjected to a geological segregation. When I first moved north, in the benighted days before our current perfection, Lexingtonians still mentioned, in hushed tones, mountain hollows narrower and darker than their prejudices, where scofflaws neither white nor black nor red lived and interbred and gave the lie to race codes dictating who could marry whom, and who was what race, and how many generations it took to flush the taint of black or red or yellow from a whitewashed family tree. All this assumed you could trust the fidelity of women willing to sleep with what was neither white nor black nor red, but something other—brass ankle, brown, redbone, mulatto, quadroon, octoroon—in the weird calculus of a racism parsing your great grandmother's genes. Even all-men-are-created-equal's Thomas Jefferson mused over his own children, as if they were cans of paint, which by addition of one drop of this or that might be labeled Hemmings's henna, Tom's tan, Virginia vanity, Monticello mulatto.

Well, of course these people inhabited godforsaken hollows steep enough and dark enough to conjure trolls. The valley's sweet lime meadows were no place for such riffraff, though over the years both sides came to believe the myth that rugged individualists chose to live where no one could grow rich, on land so intent on running up and down it never lay flat long or wide enough to make a meadow, where a million years of wearing down had buried limestone under a rumpled blanket of acid detritus that grew more rocks than crops. Capitalism's cruel calculus of success ensured that good lands went to good families, bad lands to families gone bad, accommodating the instant social registering we all engage in when, meeting someone for the first time, we note where that person lives and thereby enter him on rungs below or above our own on the invisible ladder of propriety we all carry on our shoulders—me but the latest Leland in a multigenerational slide toward mediocrity and worse.

Meanwhile the good white folk subdivided the broad and fertile valley lands among themselves, claiming first-come, first-served squatters' rights, and elbowed out to North Carolina, Kentucky, the mountains and their hollows, those who followed them. The valley porches were then and now made for watching those who travel what various generations have called the Great Warriors' Trail, "the Great Road from the Yadkin River thro Virginia to Philadelphia," U.S. 11 and Interstate 81, whose passing tires sing us lullabies throughout the night. Not that everyone yells "Get along, move along" to passersby entranced by the Shenandoah's beauty; the current plague of mcmansions sprouting from every mountaintop and mountainside betrays the sad fact that many of us would sell our very birthplaces for a dollar down and a mess of potage. Rockbridge County got its start when Thomas Fairfax, Sixth Lord Fairfax of Cameron, who owned more than five million acres of Virginia, gave Benjamin Borden rights to one hundred thousand acres on the James River, if he could settle it. Settle it he did, although court records and county gossip suggest he and his son were hardly more reliable than later generations of speculators, whom generations of county residents have learned were as ignorant of geology as they were of economics. Indians had for centuries so often fired the valley that large swathes were treeless meadows, tree-girt Brushy Hill and Timber Ridge rising like islands from a sea of grass. And early settlers mistakenly thought these hills richer land than the meadows so that they preferred settling Timber Ridge to what was better land along Hays Creek.

Later land lovers made even worse decisions fueled by iron deposits that in they dreamed might give rise to a second Birmingham, Alabama. Benjamin C. Moomaw sandwiched his 1890 dream town on thirteen thousand acres between the Blue Ridge and the Maury [then North] River, complete with opera house, hotel, and court house. The same year, Virginia Governor Fitzhugh Lee dreamed a 125-foot-wide main street and 200-room hotel near where Maury meets the

James River. And an optimistic Goshen Land and Improvement Company surveyed in 1890 some nine thousand lots at the juncture of the Calfpasture River and Mill Creek for the "Iron Centre of America." A century later, Moomaw's Buena Vista held 6,346 "happy citizens and 3 old grouches," Lee's Glasgow 1,046, and Goshen 406. Iron ore and the iron horse fueled and failed the dreams, whose backers' factory fantasies faded when America woke to the nightmare Panic of 1893, an economic depression, double digit unemployment, bank failures, and a tanking real-estate market.

However dismal their founders' financial failures, the three towns boast some of the valley's most spectacular views—and floods. Lexington, planted where Gilbert Campbell's ford crosses the Maury River, rises high enough that damage today is generally to its bridge and riverside park, especially since the town moved its sewer plant out of the floodplain. Downstream, Buena Vista and Glasgow, lying low in their rivers' floodplains, have had to learn to swim, the former even constructing a three-mile flood wall which, while keeping Buena Vista's feet dry, hurries flood waters downstream to Glasgow and beyond. Though far upstream, Goshen too suffers periodically from streams unwilling to behave, sending her flotsam down the Maury to lodge against the bridge at Lexington, the flood wall in Buena Vista, and front lawns in Glasgow. Records chronicle the floods of 1870, 1896, 1906, 1936, 1949, 1969, 1972, 1985, 1995, 1996, 2003. Older Rockbridge residents still blanch at the name of Camille, the 1969 hurricane that killed 23 people and 150 head of cattle and flooded Buena Vista with six feet of water, Glasgow with fourteen.

And still a flood of people inundates this valley, all seeking a beauty that their search destroys. Today's economic downturn conjures hope in some residents' souls that the current plague of Yankee retirees might be abated. So thought the Egyptians when the first Hyksos appeared, the Romans when Attila sent his agents westward, the Caribs when Columbus's white sails appeared one autumn morning, the Monacans when John Smith's soldiers landed. But locust plagues seldom end merely at a wish. These latest invasives squat buzzardlike upon the highest hills money can buy, lamenting the family-farm carcasses their planned communities slay. That the hilltops are free to be developed is due to geology. Both the Indians and early settlers chose lower lands to build on, since they more level, more sheltered, and closer to water. Few are the old farm houses without a permanent spring nearby, and fewer the transplants willing to use a spring as water source. For them, a well's the thing, and such wells, hundreds of feet deep, require technology unavailable till recently, so that hilltops, once upon a time, were blessedly free of fungal mcmansions.

Freer still of development are the national forests flanking the valley east and west. Refuges from what passes for hustle and bustle among Lexington's 6,800 residents, some of these woods were treeless industrial wastes a hundred years ago; charcoalers felled the forests to make fuel for area iron furnaces whose massive chimneys stand still, while the many pits miners dug excavating iron ore slowly fill with dirt and leaf. The Blue Ridge and the Alleghenies both have feet of iron, and the curious can explore the ruins of the mines, furnaces, and forges that sprang up along both. Communities along South River took their names from their industrial roles: Cornwall, like England's southwestern peninsula, was the home of tin miners, and Vesuvius's furnace suggests parallels with Italy's volcano. Today hikers in the ten thousand-acre roadless St. Mary's Wilderness "for a brief time at least, leave behind the machinery of our civilization," according to the United States Forest Service, although the Service adds that "the Saint Mary's River gorge was mined for manganese ore and iron ore until the mines were abandoned in the 1950s" and that a railroad ran where hikers now stumble. Such forests can inspire even the glummest valley resident with hope: if a mere fifty years can erase the legacy of mines and logging, who knows what the valley might look like if somehow, someway we ran out everyone for half a century and started over, this time with less of an eye toward geological segregation.

〽 MASSANUTTEN

Satellite photos reveal the Valley of Virginia to be but a part of the long curve of the Appalachians snaking up the east coast of North America and, from celestial heights, no more the Valley of Virginia than it is the Valley of Maryland, Pennsylvania, New York, Connecticut, Massachusetts, or any other state whose lands climb what space clearly reveals to be the narrow barrier that we know down South as the Blue Ridge but that masquerades under various names elsewhere. That narrow barrier stymied westward settlement in colonial Virginia, and not until 1716, more than a hundred years after Jamestown's founding, did Virginia's royal governor, Alexander Spottswood, lead a band of men up the headwaters of the Rappahannock River and cross the Blue Ridge at Swift Run Gap to view the Shenandoah, which the expedition named the Euphrates. Where Spottswood descended, the valley reaches round the southern end of Massanutten Mountain, along whose flanks run the north and south forks of the Shenandoah River, and west of which the valley opens up into a broad and rolling landscape. Its western edge marks the beginnings of the Allegheny Mountains, ridge after ridge rising in a tangle still difficult to penetrate and nearly impossible two hundred years ago, so that the Shenandoah Valley became a highway for adventurous colonists drifting south and west to and through it.

The mountains hemming in the Shenandoah Valley still determine residents' orientations, which are decidedly up valley and down valley. Lynchburg may be thirty-two miles away and Roanoke forty-five from Lexington, but those thirty-two miles are gone and beyond east of the Blue Ridge, and it's a brave soul who regularly journeys through the James River water gap, while Roanoke's an easy forty-five miles up valley, and many a Lexingtonian thinks nothing of an afternoon jaunt there. Staunton too lies a brief thirty-five miles in the other direction, down valley, but the twenty-eight miles to Clifton Forge take you west over North Mountain to hinterlands best not thought of. That Interstate 64 makes Clifton Forge an easy half an hour's drive cannot erase the psychic knowledge that North Mountain lies between you and your destination. Back before Henry Ford, climbing the mountain was a chore for man and beast, and you could spend the night at the mountain's foot, were you of a mind to do so, after riding the twelve miles

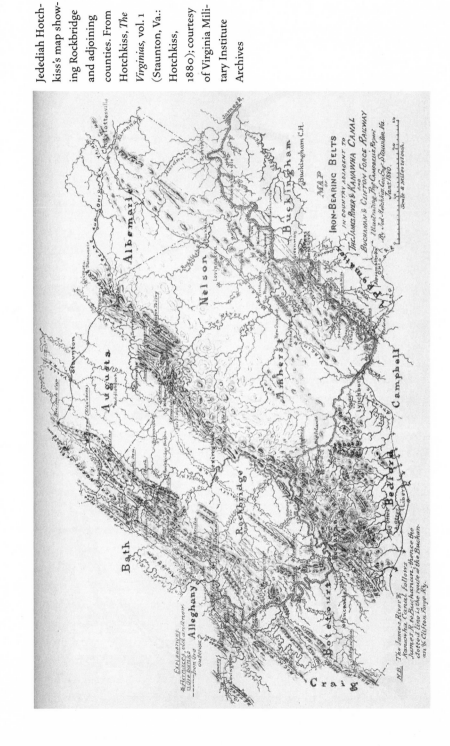

Jedediah Hotchkiss's map showing Rockbridge and adjoining counties. From Hotchkiss, *The Virginias*, vol. 1 (Staunton, Va.: Hotchkiss, 1880); courtesy of Virginia Military Institute Archives

there from Lexington—a twelve miles I think nothing of biking out and back on a Saturday morning.

But when Confederate general Thomas "Stonewall" Jackson asked his chief cartographer, Jedediah Hotchkiss, to "make me a map of the Valley," he had on his mind things more important than bike and shopping jaunts. He had war, and Hotchkiss's maps provided Jackson with the topographical details he needed to wage his 1862 valley campaign. The valley was Virginia's breadbasket, its wheat and cattle feeding General Robert E. Lee's Army of Northern Virginia. For the Yankees, the valley was a royal road to Richmond, up which an army might march unseen by Lee's forces on the other side of the Blue Ridge and so surprise him, which made the valley worth both seizing and defending. Jackson did the latter, he and his seventeen thousand men outmaneuvering and outfighting the Union troops, keeping them from attacking Richmond, and assuring Jackson's fame as one of history's great military tacticians.

And his campaign is all about topography, Jackson using the mountains that so confine valley thought, as he counseled, to "mystify, mislead, and surprise the enemy." In March of 1862, with a Union army in Fredericksburg east of the Blue

General Thomas "Stonewall" Jackson, Winchester, Virginia, 1862. Courtesy of Virginia Military Institute Archives

Ridge, another at the head of the valley in Winchester, and yet a third west of North Mountain, Jackson marched north along the Valley Pike, where U.S. 11 today runs, toward Winchester, outside of which he lost a battle but won the campaign by drawing sixty thousand federal troops away from Richmond. Retreating back up the Valley Pike, Jackson feinted east around the southern tip of Massanutten Mountain, then headed west through Staunton and North Mountain to McDowell, where he repelled a Union attack in early May. Two weeks later, he left a cavalry unit in the valley to trick the Yankees into thinking he was still there, while he crossed Massanutten into Luray Valley and marched so quickly north along the South Fork of the Shenandoah that his troops were nicknamed foot cavalry. He surprised and defeated the Union troops at Front Royal and, two days later, at Winchester as well. Alarmed, the Lincoln administration ordered twenty thousand Union troops to cross the Blue Ridge, combine with troops crossing from west of North Mountain, and cut Jackson off at Massanutten's northern end. Jackson returned south along the Valley Pike, pursued by two armies, one following him along the Valley Pike, the other on the other side of Massanutten, hoping to catch him at the southern end. There, in two battles, Jackson once again defeated the Yankees, who withdrew, leaving the valley to the Rebels for the moment and letting Jackson escape over the Blue Ridge where Interstate 64 crosses today.

If the running about confuses you, imagine what it was like back in the summer of 1862. The point, though, is the mountains, parallel ranges running north and south that let Jackson mystify, mislead, and surprise his enemy. Without Massanutten, who knows what might have happened. Today's Valley Pike is Interstate 81, which runs so close to Massanutten you can almost see Jackson's scouts standing atop its rock outcrops, counting traffic. At Woodstock, the road up and over Massanutten was there in Jackson's day. At the top, there's a tower Edward and I climb to gaze upon "the Seven Bends of the Shenandoah," the North Fork looping lazily north through the valley toward Winchester, and the Yankee columns chasing us and Jackson southward. Biographers claim George Patton imagined much the same thing as a college freshman at Jackson's school, the Virginia Military Institute. And Erwin Rommel toured the valley specifically to work out Jackson's valley campaign. He and Patton both no doubt profited from Jackson's tactics in their tank attacks across North Africa in World War II. So I don't feel too terribly silly playing war games with Edward, though I keep them from my cadets and colleagues, who think such daydreams inappropriate for English teachers.

William Washington's painting of the ruins at the Virginia Military Institute after the Civil War, with House Mountain in the background. Courtesy of Virginia Military Institute Archives

Hotchkiss made map after map of Virginia and, while nothing's quite the same as holding the real thing in your hands, thanks to the Library of Congress you can run an electronic finger over the same maps Jackson would have perused and wonder how he did it. Or match Hotchkiss's roads and rivers to today's topo maps, and plot your own hike or bike along roads once trod by armies blue and gray. Hotchkiss mapped Rockbridge County in the 1860s, and I can while away long evenings learning what the place I live in looked like 150 years ago, when H. Horn lived in the farm house near Cedar Grove on the back road to Staunton along which VMI graduate and professor and Confederate general John Mc-Causland marched his ragtag army of 1,500 men in June 1864, skirmishing with pursuing Yankees. Both Rebel and Yankee armies camped at Cedar Grove, and, some claim, both commandeered Horn's house.

The Yankees chasing McCausland were one column of an army led by General David Hunter, riding south along the Valley Pike. Hunter had been in South Carolina, where, an ardent abolitionist, he enlisted blacks into the Union army and declared months before Lincoln all slaves free in the states under his command, so angering Confederate president Jefferson Davis that he ordered Hunter killed if captured. I can trace Hunter's pursuit of McCausland on Hotchkiss's map of Rockbridge County and see where McCausland followed what are today Virginia highways 252 and 39 to Lexington, where the pursuing Yankees crossed the North [now Maury] River upstream from Cedar Grove to flank McCausland, and where Hunter followed, a few miles away, on today's U.S. Highway 11. The Yankee columns came together at Lexington, where geology dictated the Valley Pike would cross North River, for at Lexington, two creeks converge, having worn a broad passage through the cliffs of the Maury, down whose sixty-foot heights cadets rappel. Here herds of buffalo had forded, pursued by Indians, whose Great Warriors' Trail became in time "the Great Road from the Yadkin River thro Virginia to Philadelphia," the main road south for European colonists, and, in 1864, the path that Hunter followed. McCausland burned the covered wooden bridge over the North River, whose limestone abutments still stand in today's riverside park, and placed sharpshooters and a cannon along the cliffs. North of the river, Hunter stationed his men on what to this day is called Hunter's Ridge, probably in the woods behind where today the county high school's cross-country team practices. Though impressively abrupt, the cliffs where McCausland's army hid are lower that the ridge where Hunter placed his artillery, and the fight was a foregone conclusion. McCausland's men killed three or four Union soldiers before withdrawing, while Hunter's artillery bombarded the Virginia Military Institute and the town of Lexington. You can still see two of Hunter's cannonballs, stuck in the restored brickwork of the VMI barracks, three stories high, looking more like the dumbbells they really are than unexploded munitions they purport to be.

On June 12 Hunter burned the school and thus ensured the lasting hatred of VMI alumni. The school itself had won fame among southerners as Stonewall Jackson's place of employment, the nursery of hundreds of Confederate officers, and its cadets had, just the month before, distinguished themselves in the Battle of New Market, in the valley north of their school. According to the VMI surgeon's report, the school was sacked and burned at "the hands of Yankee thieves and incendiaries," while Hunter claimed the bombardment was necessary because of the "unsoldierly and inhuman attempt of General McCausland to defend an indefensible position against an overwhelming force by screening himself behind the private dwellings of women and children." Hunter's cousin, David Hunter Strother, advised the destruction since VMI was, in his words, "a place where treason was systematically taught," advice which makes his name a dirty word to this day among some Virginians; yet fellow officer and future president Rutherford B. Hayes's opposition to the burning has done little to improve his reputation among Americans northern or southern.

Hunter's abolitionist zeal was exacerbated by Confederate bushwhackers who attacked his troops and then blended into the civilian population. In West Virginia bushwhackers tied six of his men to a fence and slit their throats. In Lexington, after Hunter discovered what he described as "a violent and inflammatory proclamation from John Letcher, lately Governor of Virginia, inciting the population of the country to rise and wage a guerrilla warfare on my troops . . . I ordered his property to be burned under my order, published May 24, against persons practicing or abetting such unlawful and uncivilized warfare." Hunter's May order warned that "for every train fired upon, or soldier of the Union wounded or assassinated by bushwhackers in any neighborhood within the reach of my command, the houses and other property of every secession sympathizer residing within a circuit of five miles from the place of the outrage, shall be destroyed by fire." Incensed Confederates sought revenge, and General Jubal Early found it on July 30, when he had McCausland give Chambersburg, Pennsylvania, residents a choice: cough up one hundred thousand dollars in gold or your town burns. It burned.

Driving north on today's highways, you pass Chambersburg, where an historical marker was my introduction to this sordid moment in American history. These highways trace the northern reaches of the Valley Pike Jackson so brilliantly maneuvered on and the route on which Hunter rode south toward VMI and McCausland traveled north to Pennsylvania. Many a beer I've drunk while listening to older residents' remembering their fathers' remembering their fathers' remembering. I've talked with Civil War reenactors whose passion for battles six generations gone drives them to dress like escapees from the nineteenth century. And with cadets who march north along U.S. Highway 11 to New Market, where ten of their number died one summer's day so long ago it seems just yesterday. And with cadets from the North who mock our memories, and with cadets from Thailand and Taiwan who comprehend them not. Above us all rise Massanutten and North mountains and the Blue Ridge, beautiful, enduring, and indifferent to the human quarrels whose fates they shape.

〰 FOREST COMMUNITIES

At certain seasons House Mountain looks as if its forests were arranged by color. In summer, the mountain is draped in green, but, come fall, this blanket shreds into arthritic fingers of green reaching valleyward against a yellow backdrop. Guidebooks confirm such color schemes, dividing the forest into distinct plant communities: the green fingers, ridge-growing, pine-oak forest communities, and the yellow- backdrop, valley-hugging, oak-hickory communities. These are typical, the books, say of drier, southwest facing slopes of the Appalachians.

Europeans sought to discover the mysteries of such plant associations by laboriously counting individual plants in randomly chosen plots. Certain plants, such as beeches and maples, repeatedly formed communities. Americans noticed the same thing, among them Frederick Clements, who argued that these associations could be viewed as if they were themselves organisms with births, lives, and deaths, and that they gave way, one to the other, in an orderly succession tending toward a climax forest that would, undisturbed, last forever.

I remember being taught the term *climax forest*, and a part of me still seeks it, driving hours to walk through postage stamp-sized remnants of what I imagine was the great and near eternal American forest that predated European settlement. Anyone who has watched an abandoned field grow up knows that succession is real, that annual weeds arrive first, only to be supplanted by perennial herbs in a few years that then give way to weedy shrubs and briars that eventually give way to trees. Here in the Valley of Virginia such succession is the bane of farmers who, to maintain pasture, must mow their fields on a regular basis to keep down weeds. But such tedious mowing is a catch-as-catch-can proposition, done in between more pressing jobs, so that the farmer who rented our fields seldom mowed before late fall. By that time, the stickweed and thistle had already set seed. So I took to walking the fields in midsummer when their flowers were new, beheading legions of massed stickweed, thistle after thistle falling with a satisfying thwack to my swingblade. But the upwind fields across Cedar Creek bloomed yellow with stickweed, and our neighbor's paddocks were chockablock with Canada thistle already downing up for the flight into our fields. And thistle itself resprouts, as do the red cedars and shoestring the farmer would later brush hog so that our labors but prepared us for more next year. We were vainly trying to stop time itself, a process the Indians began when they maintained the valley's grasslands by repeatedly firing them. You can tell roughly how long ago a farmer gave up fighting time by what's growing in his fields—stickweed is always present, but broomgrass and shoelace vine suggest abandonment several years before, while multiflora and cedar thickets take years to develop. And many a deciduous forest has remnant cedars and locusts that betray its origin as an open field.

But what sort of forest? Am I right in thinking that the nascent oak and hickory forests climbing up House Mountain's flanks are the natural inheritors of the land, that their restitution represents a return to a primitive purity? Not really. Science tells us that such forests are only ten thousand or so years old around here, that before this, back when the land was cold, boreal forests like those in Canada dominated the landscape, and that House Mountain's summit and upper flanks were, in all probability, treeless. Remnants of this boreal forest, which lasted for millennia, came into their own in West Virginia, where many were logged into extinction a hundred years ago. Spruce Knob, 4,863 feet high, sports an alpine forest of wind-tortured red spruce similar to what might have clung to House Mountain's lower slopes during the last Ice Age, which began about seventy thousand years ago and ended only ten thousand years ago. West Virginia's Cranberry Glades preserve a flora of spruce, mountain ash, huckleberry, and cranberry more like those in Canada and the last Ice Age than like those in the sunny South of the Shenandoah Valley. Indeed, only twenty miles from Lexington are bogs where wild cranberries grow, thought to be leftovers from the same Ice Age. Few people visit them, so there are plenty of cranberries for Thanksgiving, if you're willing to risk cold feet.

The oak-hickory forest association I walk through today is itself the product of European interference, since only a hundred years ago the dominant tree here would have been the chestnut, whose demise thanks to an imported fungus is told and retold as an ecological cautionary tale. One out of every four trees in the Appalachians was once a chestnut; today, fewer than one hundred large chestnut trees survive. One of these grows just over the Blue Ridge in Amherst County. The stumps of the last of Rockbridge County's native chestnuts still dot House Mountain's lower flanks; most are small, second- or third-growth trees, all cut off at nearly the same level, suggesting the landowners hereabouts cut down their chestnuts as the end came in order to make something off the dying and dead trees. Some chestnuts still try to raise a trunk, but these are all shrubby affairs, their succession of dead trunks testifying to the lethality of the fungus, whose embrace reveals itself in circles of burst bark. If the oak-chestnut-hickory association were anything other than adventitious, wouldn't the sudden and universal demise of the chestnut have had more effect than it did? As far as the dominant trees were concerned, the chestnut die-off merely allowed hickories the opportunity to become more prevalent. And numbers suggest that deer and turkey and squirrels found plenty to replace the once abundant chestnuts themselves.

So too our children survive, despite their parents' divorces, my son, Edward, thriving, though his associations now not those I fantasized upon his birth and shaded by men other than myself. Likewise, those who ring the Shenandoah forests' death knell may be burying that which will live, though altered far from that we knew or wished. Certainly, the forests as we know them are endangered; the chestnut is as good as gone and with it its attendant weevils, moths, and butterflies; the alien woolly adelgid threatens the native hemlock and, with it, the trout it shades in mountain streams; and fungus extirpates the understory dogwood in all but the sunniest of locales. As undesirable as they may be, however, foreign plants are as happy to fill the emptying niches of our eastern forests as suitors are to fill my ex-wife's empty evenings. Trees of heaven are as common as cedars in much of the Shenandoah; the paulownia or princess tree blooms on many a mountain roadside; kudzu is legendary in the South, itself threatened with replacement in the popular mind by aggressive mile-a-minute vines. Though we may not like these aliens, they have actually increased the number of species growing in America, and as many as 30 percent of the plants in many states are foreign.

These have all found homes here thanks to humans. But how did chestnuts, oaks, and hickories climb the slopes of House Mountain if the Ice Age exiled them to warmer, lower refuges? All their fruits are too heavy to move far on their own, and none is likely to roll uphill. But ten thousand generations of foraging squirrels, burying and forgetting their harvests, can move, if not mountains, then trees up mountains, and it is they who are thought to have wrought this slow miracle of reclothing the Appalachian Mountains. But it was slow work, so slow that the heavier chestnut lagged behind the lighter acorn and had not made it into northern New England by the time of its settlement by Europeans.

If, then, the oak-chestnut-hickory association is merely one of happenstance, what might the future forests of this region look like? As easily, perhaps, describe my future loves or yours. However, given the onslaught of global warming, the trees that grow here in the future will no doubt be more southern than northern. Already the northern remnants of the Ice Age are under siege: trapped on the low-altitude mountains on which they grow, they cannot retreat northward to Canada and so are forced ever higher up the slopes of the mountains on which they survive, clinging precariously to these fragments of boreal climate even as the temperature rises. Virginia's highest peak, Mount Rogers, now clothed in a view-choking subalpine forest of red spruce and Fraser fir, may soon be bare because of acid rain and global warming. That it makes a popular Christmas tree insures the Frazier's survival, if only in plantations. The same evils also threaten the range-restricted Carolina hemlock, a southern version of the more wide-spread Canada hemlock.

Neither of these trees grows naturally in Rockbridge County, our elevation being too low. But House and the other nearby mountains do shelter trees normally found much farther north. The Appalachians provide a narrow spine of northern climate that penetrates as far south as Georgia, and many northern species, or close relatives adapted to the Appalachians, grow here. So, when I climb House or North Mountain, I keep an eye out for small green trunks with white stripes, the telltale mark of the moosewood, a tree which, as its name suggests, is more at home in Canada than Virginia but which grows as far south as northern Georgia, having snaked its way south along the mountains millennia ago. Moosewood will grow in the valley—I transplanted a small sapling once—but it cannot compete with more favored plants, preferring instead the colder heights of our mountains. So I know I have left the valley behind when I spot moosewood in the understory. But moosewood will go when global warming comes.

In its place others will emerge. People have planted sweet gums throughout the valley, but none, so far, has reproduced from seed. Loblolly pine plantations have sprouted in the valley, even though the tree is native only to the eastern half of Virginia. Live oaks, whose northernmost expression is the Eastern Shore of Virginia, hang on precariously in Lexington, and I have even managed to coax dwarf palmetto seeds to sprout. They grow a year or two but then succumb to our cold winters. Perhaps, with global warming, Edward will grow palmettos in Lexington.

Though plainly evident from Lexington, House Mountain's green, arthritic fingers prove more elusive closer up. Climbing the road to the saddle, I veer off cross-country on one of the many pine-clothed ridges that work their way steeply uphill. While I can stand on the ridge and recognize I am in a predominately pine woods, or I can walk a hundred feet downslope to a cove and stand in a tulip grove, just where the one gives way to the other is impossible to decide. No sharp line divides these two distinct communities; rather, they merge slowly one into the other, and the multicolored communities I see from town dissolve into a confused tangle when I stand on House Mountain's flanks.

But so too do our lives. Read most biographies and you'd think humanity all Dorothy's in Oz, our black and white childhood worlds abruptly becoming colored adulthood with the opening of a door. Even the Bible supposes lives lived in radically different befores and afters, Adam and Eve falling from Eden, Jesus rising baptized from the Jordan. My life's more a muddle: forty years from childhood, I've still got half a foot in primary school, and the climax forest of adulthood at times seems as distant now as ever it was. "Ancient of days," my stepson calls me, in the tones of a logger estimating how many board feet he can get from some forest monarch in whose shade he stands; but I feel more a sapling in disguise, measuring myself as I do against the great ones of my youth. And though the world to me seems filled with second-growth people as well as forests, we and they, in our turn, will seem primeval to our children's children.

CEDARS

When we first got our sweaters out of mother's cedar chest fifty years ago in the fall, they smelled of cedar as we put them on. To me the scent of cedar is a Norman Rockwell memory of fall and mother and childhood. Happily for me cedars are weeds in Virginia, so many growing along fence rows and in abandoned fields that their farmers are happy for me to cut my Christmas tree on their land. Edward and I go out armed with an ax, and we examine far too many trees, opining as to their size and bulk and color and texture, me naysaying the twelve-foot monsters my nine-year-old thinks perfect until we settle on a more reasonably sized tree. We take turns chopping and, as the fates and a little fudging on my part have it, it is always Edward who finally fells the tree.

While Edward sizes up Christmas trees, I enjoy the variety that a grove of cedars provides, each tree a different shade of green, from truly green to almost blue, some upright and columnar, others broad and blowsy, some wispy, almost weeping. Cedars are dioecious, either male or female, and the females sport tiny berries that are deep blue when ripe and a mainstay for wild birds during deep winter—thus explaining the ubiquity of cedars. The males have miniature cones on the tips of their branches, which turn the trees a brownish hue in spring and are so loaded with pollen that trees "smoke" when you shake their branches.

They are among the first trees to colonize a field, and farmers must bush hog their fields to rid themselves of these nuisances. In Nebraska they're classed as an invasive weed. Walk a valley field and you'll find hundreds of inch-high stubborn cedars reaching prickly stubs toward the light. Before mechanization, farmers fired their fields, and before farming, the Indians fired their prairies, cedars not discriminating in whom they plague. Left to grow, they're plagued in turn. Among the most noticeable of their enemies is the bagworm (*Thyridopteryx ephemeraeformis*), a moth whose larva feeds on them and other trees while living within a silken cocoon camouflaged with half-inch-long snippets of leaves. When grown, the male pupates within his cocoon and then emerges to find a female and mate, often leaving the brownish husk of his now empty pupa sticking out of the bottom of the cocoon. The female lives and dies within hers, leaving a small knot you can feel if you rub one between your fingers. A perennial pest, bagworms can so infest a tree that they defoliate it, leaving their nearly indestructible bags hanging like so many Christmas ornaments from their host.

Less noticeable is the cedar apple rust fungus, *Gymnosporangium juniperi-virginianae*, which looks like a purplish brown misshapen golf ball glued to a branch for the two years it takes to mature. Come maturity and spring rains, it blooms, and aliens invade the cedars, infesting their branches with otherworldly, hydra-headed, orange-tentacled, gelatinous balls. The gall-like "cedar balls" or "apples" swell and grow dozens of tentacles, each several inches long, and each filling the air with microscopic spores blown higgledy-piggledy, the lucky few falling on and infecting by mere chance the leaves and fruit of apple trees. The first sign of infection is generally discoloration in the leaves, which eventually develop rusty colored circles on their undersides. When these mature at the end of summer, they discharge their spores by the million and reinfect the cedar trees. Apple trees infected by the fungus sport misshapen fruit and often weaken and die. Cedar trees, however, appear to suffer little damage.

Before commercial orchards became widespread in the valley following the Civil War, what we know as cedar apple rust was perceived as two unrelated pests, apple rust and cedar rust. Not until 1888 did scientists discover the two were one. Growers ignored the benefits of extirpating cedar trees near apple orchards until an especially disastrous outbreak of cedar apple rust in 1912 led them to ask the state's legislature to do something. That something was a 1914 law allowing apple growers to fell all cedar trees within a one-mile (later broadened to two-mile) radius of their fields. Most neighbors cooperated with the efforts to stop the yo-yoing fungus. But an outraged few who had cedar groves or avenues objected to the state's refusal to compensate their aesthetic losses. One New Market, Virginia, resident's appeals went all the way to the U.S. Supreme Court, which ruled in 1928 in favor of the state.

A similar West Virginia law led cedar lovers there to appeal to then President Herbert Hoover to spare their trees. Property owners in Shepherdstown draped their cedars with American flags in a vain attempt to save the trees, and Serena Dandridge threw herself in front of the last of five hundred cedars on her property, daring the lumbermen to chop her down. But apple orchardists won the day; as the secretary to the West Virginia Horticultural Society pointed out in the *New York Times*, West Virginia's Eastern Panhandle was home to thirty thousand acres of commercial orchards which brought in four million dollars annually. Not until after World War II were effective fungicides developed that kept the rust in check.

Today orchard growers rely on spraying where their ancestors eighty years ago relied on clear-cutting.

Thus cedar lovers like Serena Dandridge can keep their groves these days, not that there are many in these parts, most farmers more intent on clearing them from their land than remarking on their beauty. Cedars can live to be three hundred years old, sixty feet high and two feet thick. I used to climb one half that thick when I was a boy. It stood in an old field and had retained its lower branches so that a boy could easily make his way from branch to branch up, up, and away into the treetop from where it seemed he might see forever. Hundreds of dead branches lined my route, pencil thin stubs that had lost out in the race for sun and which broke easily, filling the air and my nostrils with the scent of cedar. The thick-sown cedars of most fields, however, lose their lower branches as they fight their neighbors for sunlight, so that a cedar grove is often filled with tall, straight, slender trees, and littered with the rot-resistant bodies of those that lost the fight for light and life. Like many conifers, cedars concentrate their aromatic oils in their heartwood, conferring near immortality upon their woody carcasses, which may be all that remain sixty or seventy years after the last live cedar died in a now deciduous forest. Moss-shrouded and gray, these knotty stumps and boles, if cut open, are still blood red within, seem almost alive, and fill the air with essence of cedar.

Various cedars grow throughout the continental United States and are, technically, not cedars at all, but junipers. So the cedar of the Shenandoah Valley, the eastern red cedar, is really *Juniperus virginiana,* and it is ubiquitous in the valley, whose limestones provide the tree the calcium it loves. Valley mountains are erosion-resistant, acidic sandstones, which cedars find unpalatable, so that a rough guide to the substrate you're walking on is the presence of cedars— provided you're not in a forest. Cedars are intolerant of shade, and if you are in a forest and come upon mature cedars or their rot-resistant carcasses, you're probably looking at evidence that what is now a forest was once a field.

Which is what House Mountain's lower slopes once were. From Lexington, House looks like one mountain, but it is, in fact, two, separated by a saddle, a Bali-Hai surprise of an apple orchard planted within a forest. Geologists tell us that Sugar and Kerr's creeks have breached the resistant sandstone cap of House Mountain, wearing away the less resistant limestones beneath. Right though the scientists are, the heart believes the saddle a jeu d'esprit of a generous god, who thought that here, yes, here, we need a secret vale. Sir Arthur Conan Doyle located his atop mesas in South America; H. Rider Haggard discovered his beyond the

Kalahari; and James M. Barrie found his "second star to the right and straight on till morning." Mine is more down to earth.

I am among those whom House Mountain feeds, first come, first served, to all in the know and neighborhood. Deer beat all else to both apples and leaves within neck-stretching range, the orchard wearing that groomed-from-the-bottom-up look cow-filled fields take on. Higher, apples remain for Edward and his friends to scamper up the boughs and pick, shake, jiggle, jump as many down as we are willing to backpack home. "Magnified apples appear and disappear, / Stem end and blossom end," wizened, pockmarked, and worm infested, but better than Kroger's, if only by the hike up to get them. The illusion that we are connecting with our pioneer ancestors, reenacting a ritual as old as Robert Frost's lends flavors no supermarket can compete with, bring their apples from the antipodes though they do.

Nowadays they bush hog to keep the orchard open. But years ago, they fired the mountain. Lexington native and Princeton theologian Archibald Alexander remembered watching it burn at night in the 1730s: "a long crooked string along the side of the mountain ... a zig-zag fire in the sky." At Smokey's behest, we have prevented forest fires, and the only time I've watched the mountains burn was after a careless hunter threw his cigarette away on Jump Mountain. A hundred weary firefighters did their damnedest to keep me from seeing, but hidden fire crept up out of Goshen Pass and over the long, slow slope of Jump, an orange delight writhing in the night, so many *Gymnosporangium* tongues licking their ways down the mountain to where, sadly but thankfully, they burnt out. But they converted me in their decay into a pyromaniac, who, here in House Mountain's secret saddle, can pass the night with a fire of apple bough and cedar branch, warming myself over the hydra-tentacled remembrance of fungal infection.

House Mountain's outskirts are rickracked with fence rows green in cedar. But the trails up soon forsake cedars for other trees. Here and there stand long dead cedars whose shaggy limbed silhouettes tell another story, that these were once fields which, abandoned, sprouted cedars that grew until senescence let their deciduous rivals overtake and overshade them, and, one by one, they died.

They grow Christmas trees all along the Appalachians' spine, and I could get myself far trimmer trees than that Edward and I harvest out of my friend's pasture. All the formal perfection I can buy, however, pales before the pleasure of taking my boy into the field the way my father took me and letting him select our family tree—double trunked, misshapen, too tall, and way too wide, but ours. Edward hands me a wood chip and tells me to smell it. "Cedar, Dad; it smells good." May his child, thirty years from now, do the same to him.

MAPLE SYRUP

Upstream from its buried life, Sugar Creek behaves like a good mountain creek should, splashing along on a limestone creek bed from pool to riffle to pool, none deep enough for you to do much more than wade around in, chase minnows and water striders, and keep an eye out for snakes and turtles. The cobbles grow imperceptibly larger as you hike up creek, and at some point near Robert Carter's farm, you realize they become boulders and the creek is having trouble making its way between the increasingly angular rock choking its bed, which has left the fields for the woods, and hemlocks have begun to darken the sky and water, and there's a chill even in August, and you feel that you're not really in Rockbridge County any more, but somewhere farther north, somewhere where cold-loving trees grow and it's never really ever hot, and House Mountain begins to loom overhead in a worrisome sort of way that makes you also realize that the creek may be descending but you are climbing and at a fast rate.

There's still a valley, and the people living here are doing their second-rate best to keep it open, but House Mountain makes more and more claim upon the land, which has begun to rise, rise, rise, and places flat enough for a house or shed or cow are becoming scarce. The land is littered with rock, sandstone boulders that tumbled down from higher up eons ago, back when the Ice Age gripped America and House Mountain was, in all probability, a barren, treeless tundra; its sandstone cap cracked and crumbled as water made its way into fissures, froze and expanded, melted and contracted, breaking the mountain apart bit by bit. I know if I go up high enough I'll find house-sized boulders that have rolled down House Mountain's flanks. They never made it quite this far, the rocks here the shattered fragments of those massive fragments of the mountain itself. The boulders sit in sand, itself showered down from the top of House, burying the limestone bedrock under thirty feet of acidic soil that encourages a different flora than does the valley. There in the bucolic, civilized expansiveness of the Shenandoah Valley you'll find the ubiquitous cedar tree, a weed sprouting in every field and fence and hedgerow, shat out by the birds that feast upon its berries in the winter, cursed by the farmers who have to bush hog their fields to rid them of this woody weed, blessed by children playing hide and seek in abandoned fields, home to deer and fox, and focal point of country Christmases. Here, though, the soil turning acid, the cedar grows scarce, and, if you care to, you can trace its gradual eradication as you climb from sweet valley soil to acidic mountain soil, the highest cedar that I know of perched just below the crest of the old toll road over the Allegheny, a scraggly specimen gripping the last bit of limestone beneath the first bit of Silurian sandstone. Climbing House Mountain you also can find increasingly rare cedars, old trees that sprouted sixty, seventy years ago when the lower slopes were still open and now dying off without hope of progeny, the forest canopy having closed in on them, shade killing whatever seeds sprout in the already marginal soil.

But cedars are not what made Sugar Creek Sugar Creek. Acidic soil, elevation, and a valley too steep sided to make good pasture gave Sugar Creek its name, which comes from the sugar maples that grow along its banks and up its valley sides. Here in Rockbridge County is the southern tailing off of what is farther north big business—maple syrup and sugar. We think of these as Canadian and New England, and it is true that the roots of today's sugaring industry are deepest there. But sugar maples grow as far south as Georgia, and people made maple sugar and syrup far farther south than we suppose. In his travels through colonial Carolina, John Lawson heard of "the Sugar-Tree . . . in places that are near the Mountains. . . . The Indians tap it, and make Gourds to receive the Liquor." Sugar Creek, of course, rises "in places that are near the Mountains," and so it is only fitting that it be the site of sugaring. We who buy five pounds of pure cane sugar in our grocery stores without giving its provenance a thought are quite unlike our colonial forebears, who knew all too well the costly price of sugar.

For sugar was the motive force behind slavery. As odious as America's slavery was, the West Indies' version was a thousand times more obscene. And it centered on sugar cane. So horrendous were conditions on the Caribbean sugar plantations that it was cheaper to replace dead slaves with new ones imported from Africa than to nurture and nourish the children of those already in place. North American slave markets were an afterthought to the West Indian trade. Nor need we quibble over whose hands, northern or southern, were deeper drenched in blood and bigotry; there's plenty of blame to go around. The deadly triangle of African slaves sold in the Indies for rum, sugar and molasses that were sold in the colonies southern and northern for money that bought more slaves to be sold for more rum, sugar, and molasses that made more money for more slaves. And so the obscene trade continued, and every child in North America that ever ate a cookie supported the abomination. Disgusting and dangerous, the

American balance of trade was always and forever in the red thanks to our greed for Caribbean sugar. If only there were an alternative.

Which there was. Maple sugar.

Today's maple syrup is a yuppie item, expensive as hell and not to be wasted on the kids, as least not in my household. But in colonial America, people casting about for ways to break slavery's stranglehold latched onto maple sugar. What if we replaced West Indian, slave-made sugar with the maple sugar of American farmers? Philadelphia's Quakers were the first to make much of the idea, Dr. Benjamin Rush prominent among them: "I cannot help contemplating a sugar maple tree with a species of affection and even veneration, for I have persuaded myself to behold in it the happy means of rendering the commerce and slavery of our African brethren in the Sugar Indies as unnecessary as it has always been inhuman and unjust." Encourage every farmer to plant a grove of sugar maples and America might free herself not only of an onerous foreign-trade debt but also of an even more oppressive reliance on slavery. Persuaded, Thomas Jefferson commanded only maple sugar be served at Monticello and ordered sixty trees to be planted there. Alas the trees took thirty years to reach maturity, by which time Eli Whitney had invented the cotton gin, and slavery, in service of cotton and sugar, was as American a problem as it was West Indian.

But for a few years maple sugar became as political a statement as shade-grown coffee or organic cotton are today. And about as effective. The Holland Land Company's 1791 purchase of twenty-three thousand Vermont acres upon which to grow sugar maple failed, and James Fenimore Cooper's father lost both money and prestige vainly promoting a sugar market boom in Otsego, New York. Slavery prevailed and cane sugar, grown by slave labor in the Deep South, became American. No longer did buying it contribute to the national debt, and, assuming the blood upon the bags didn't bother you, you could buy sugar with a clear conscience. Despite abolitionist attempts to make cane sugar and molasses pariah products, Americans bought them in increasing quantities. Maple sugar production peaked in 1860, which some today see as a triumph of moral consumerism but which most economic historians see as an irrelevant moment in the always increasing trajectory of sugar cane's monopolistic hold upon sugar.

Indians first taught European colonists the sugar maple's sweet properties, and those of the birch, sycamore, and other trees. But it was the sugar maple that had the highest concentration—3 to 9 percent—of sugar, and so it captured the market. Early travel accounts were compelled to include descriptions of sugaring. Hard to transport and harder to preserve, syrup could be boiled down into an easily transportable, easily preservable granular sugar. Not until late did maple syrup overtake maple sugar, by which time both had become luxury items in a market dominated by cane sugar. Sugar is what Indians made, using it mixed with corn gruel or animal fat as an energy-rich food during times of want or long journeys. Early traveler Peter Kalm reports that maple sugar was the preferred present that Indians gave when they went visiting, that the French army had learned from the Indians how to make sugar and required their soldiers to provide themselves with their own sweeteners, and that he himself subsisted on maple sugar. Virginia's royal governor William Berkeley wrote in 1706, "The Sugar-Tree yields a kind of Sap or Juice which by boiling is made into Sugar. This Juice is drawn out, by wounding the Trunk of the Tree, and placing a Receiver under the Wound. It is said that the Indians make one Pound of Sugar out of eight Pounds of the Liquor. It is bright and moist, with a full large Grain, the Sweetness of it being like that of good Muscadova."

The same process is used today. First you tap the tree, which should be at least thirty years old and eight to ten inches in diameter. Not that reasonable tapping hurts a tree. Scientific studies suggest that each tap takes, at most, 9 percent of a tree's sap, which foresters think a negligible quantity. A robust old- growth tree, it is thought, can sustain four taps without harm—although the former rapacious practice of thirty taps per tree is discouraged. On average, forty gallons of tap boil down to one gallon of syrup, and five gallons of syrup boil down to one pound of sugar. Tapping requires a hole, and any sort of drill will do, as long as it produces a hole no deeper than three inches, upward trending to prevent rainwater collection and reasonably small. In fact, any sort of slash across the bark of sugar maple will produce sap; what syrup manufacturers want is a manageable flow that doesn't harm the tree and that can be sustained for decades.

Indians probably learned of maple sugar by sucking on the slightly sweet sapsickles hanging from damaged tree branches in mid winter. What commercial producers want is to mimic this flow over several weeks. Ingenious minds have graduated from slashed bark to augered holes to elderberry pipettes to today's metal spouts or spiles, as they are called in the trade. Indians used bark and pottery containers to catch the sap; colonists used buckets; today's industrialized producers use plastic piping and suction and air-tight collectors. The sap is then boiled down, increasing the percentage of sugar. While old-fashioned sugaries use a shallow, open-faced pan over an open fire and more modern producers use enclosed, sanitary boilers, the idea is the same—reduce the amount of water to increase the percentage of sugar.

The USDA recognizes three grades of maple syrup—light, medium, and dark amber. Generally speaking, the lighter the syrup the earlier in the year it was made and the milder its flavor. Light amber syrup is the basis for most maple sugars; medium amber is the most popular for syrups. Dark amber gives the most maplely of syrups. Like you, I buy my syrup from the store. But there was a time when I bought it from a local producer, and I swear his syrup was better than anything I've tasted since. I met Dr. Brush soon after I moved to Lexington; he was selling his syrup in a local street fair and, buying two bottles, I engaged him in conversation and discovered that not only did he make the stuff himself, but he made it right here in Lexington. Next January, I walked over to Dr. Brush's home, a stately house overlooking Wood's Creek and, more importantly, surrounded by twenty or more maple trees. From each tree depended one or two spouts, three inch sections of plastic piping that Dr. Brush had stuck into holes he'd augured with a hand bit and drill. Each piece of pipe hung suspended in the mouth of a gallon plastic milk jug, drip drip dripping its sweet sap throughout the morning, Dr. Brush explaining to me as we collected the jugs that sap flow was highest in the morning on bright, sunny days following cloudless nights when the temperature plunged below freezing. We chugged around his lawn on a John Deere riding mower with wagon in tow filling with jug after jug of, to me, nearly tasteless sap. Back of the house was the family barbecue, a brick grill stoked with downed limbs from the trees we had tapped and topped with a shallow, flat pan two inches deep. Into this pan we poured jug after jug of sap, which soon commenced steaming and boiling and then foaming, all the while smelling more and more and more like a dozen broken bottles of maple syrup. Dr. Brush had me fishing out bits of branch and charcoal that drifted down into the bubbling sap, which I gladly did as I then got to lick the stick I used to fish the pieces out. When he considered that the syrup was thick enough, a mysterious moment that he never quite explained, we lifted the boiling pan off the fire and let it cool enough so that its amber liquid could be poured off into a polyglot assembly of jars.

Since then, I've been to Monterey, Virginia, and watched professionals make syrup, tasted the product and declared it worth buying. But nothing compares to the syrup we made that day, not even the pale imitation I made years later when, Dr. Brush having died, I had to beg trees from my neighbors, attaching milk jugs up and down Jefferson and Jackson and White streets in an attempt to collect enough sap to make a gallon of syrup. That's forty some gallons of sap, and I never did find enough trees, so I contented myself with boiling what I did have down into sugar, which merely meant leaving it longer on the fire, which was my kitchen stove, which meant I had a hell of a gas bill the next month and moldy walls. Later, I lived in a house with two maples that Edward and I tapped, collecting just enough sap to leave a sweet crusty residue on the pan's bottom after the liquid boiled away.

From what little I know of maple syruping, I'd say the best syrup must be made outdoors, over an open fire so that ash and smoke and God knows what all can mix with the sap and boil down into a smoky-flavored liquid thicker and darker and maplelier than any sanitary thing you can buy in the store. I also know that you can never make enough of this syrup to last the year out, so don't even try, just be a glutton and enjoy the momentary bounty. And mistakenly boil some down into sugar that you've got to scrape off the pot and spoon and that barely warrants saving, but do so anyway and give it to some one you love, preferably someone several decades younger than you so that you can addict them forever to that which they will be compelled to make themselves.

⚘ POISON IVY

We all learned from our parents or older siblings to beware leaflets three, although it takes a bout of itching to properly appreciate such cautions. And what is summer without a bout or two of poison ivy? It and its cousin poison oak are everywhere, even more plentiful today than before the arrival of Europeans, since neither does well in the thick shade of old-growth forests.

When Edward and I climb House Mountain, we guard against poison ivy, looking for its hairy vines grappling their way nearly straight up trees' trunks, its thick branches looking at first like tree limbs, and covered at summer's end with a cornucopia of small white berries, a favorite food of migrating birds, which explains poison ivy's ubiquitous presence along valley fence rows where birds rest and shit. Both berries and leaves are favorites of white-tailed deer and other browsers. No one but humans seems very allergic to the plants, although scientists have induced allergic reactions in laboratory animals by shaving their fur and dosing them with the plant's poisonous resin, urushiol, which lurks inside tiny duct glands within its stems, roots, leaves, flowers, and fruit. Easily bruised, the plant bleeds the resin, providing quick-sealing protection against invasive bacteria and virus, which is the only evolutionary explanation for the poison that Darwinists have been able to come up with.

Biblical scholars, of course, have an alternative explanation for the poison— God's cursing the land following the fall of Adam and Eve. "Cursed is the ground for thy sake; in sorrow shalt thou eat of it all the days of thy life; Thorns also and thistles shall it bring forth to thee," Genesis reports God telling our progenitors. Along with thorns and thistles we might add poison ivy. Some scientists think that poison ivies originated in North America tens of millions of years ago, spreading later to Asia and South America. While they differ on the dating, Mormons should agree with the point of origin, since Joseph Smith located the Garden of Eden in Missouri. Adam and Eve, perhaps, were the first people to suffer from poison ivy.

The plant must also have plagued Native Americans, although folklore holds that they are immune to it. Not so, say scientists, although there is some evidence that fairer-skinned people suffer more than do darker-skinned. But certain indigenous people must have known something modern Americans don't: a thirteenth-century Southwest Indian medicine bag contained poison oak seeds, as did the ruins at Mesa Verde. And Californian Indians used the plants' resin to dye their baskets and reportedly even made baskets from the stems—if you can imagine weaving freshly cut poison oak stalks with your hands.

Europeans, however, generally had little use for the plant. Virginia's Captain John Smith described it in terms that explain its common name, poison ivy: "The poisoned weed is much in shape like our English ivy, but being touched, causeth redness, itching, and lastly, blisters, and which, howsoever after a while pass away of them-selves, without further harm; yet because for the time they are somewhat painfill, it hath got itself an ill name, although questionless of no ill nature."

Incredible though it may seem, Thomas Jefferson grew it in his garden. He called it poison oak, but the folk at Monticello think he meant our poison ivy and suppose he planted it to climb up trees and provide fall color. Both poison ivy and poison oak made their way into English and Continental gardens, where they were soon enough cursed by those foolish enough to plant them. An English sea captain, Frederick Beechey, is said to have brought back poison oak from California following his 1820s voyage there, despite his having described it under its Spanish name of yedra, or ivy, as "a poisonous plant . . . producing tumours and violent inflammation upon any part with which it comes in contact; and indeed even the exhalation of it borne upon the wind, is said to have an effect upon some people." As late as 1908, it was, according to one account, still found in many English gardens. Australians now suffer from poison ivy as well, enthusiastic gardeners there having imported it for its fall foliage. And the enterprising Dutch have planted it on their dikes, providing fall color while discouraging people from climbing on and damaging the public works.

Versions of Beechey's exhalation keep cropping up in poison-ivy lore. Writing of poison sumac, which he said Americans called the poison tree, the eighteenth-century traveler Peter Kalm recorded that, "I was acquainted with a person, who, merely by the noxious exhalation of it, was swelled to such a degree, that he was as stiff as a log of wood, and was turned about in his bed." As an experiment, Kalm reported that, "I cut a branch of the tree, and carried it in my hand for about half hour together, and smelt at it now and then. But next morning I awoke with a violent itching of my eye-lids, and the parts thereabouts; and this was so painful, that I could hardly keep my hands from it." While Kalm subscribed to the then-popular notion of noxious exhalations, we suspect he had touched his eye-lids the day before with the hand that carried the sumac branch and so infected himself. Confederate botanist Francis Porcher wrote a century later in scientific-sounding prose that, "An acrimonious vapor, combined with carburetted hydrogen, exhales from a growing plant of the poison oak sumach during the night, can be collected in a jar, and is capable of inflaming and blistering the skin of persons of excitable constitution who plunge their arms into it." Today's botanists think this sinister vapor most likely an allergic reaction to a jar whose sides came into contact with the plant, not a domestic version of the deadly Upas tree of Asia, reputed to kill by vapor alone everything within a fifteen-mile radius. You can, however, catch poison ivy from smoke if you burn the plant; the smoke contains minute particles of unburned plant and its attendant poison oil. Which explains the origin of what I can only hope is urban legend, that drug dealers intent on revenge sell victims bags of dried poison ivy in lieu of marijuana.

Early accounts favored poisonous vapors as the agent behind poison ivy's toxic effects, in part because of the widespread notion that bad air was the source of much disease and contagion. As this belief waned, pollen and bacteria became the culprits. However, in the first decade of the twentieth century, Japanese scientists isolated the actual agent, an oil so powerful that a quarter of an ounce would infect everyone in the world. Determining that the poison in American poison ivies and oaks was similar to that in the Japanese lacquer tree, *Toxicodendron vernicifluum*, the scientists called the oil urushiol, after *urushi*, their name for the tree whose sap provides lacquer for Chinese, Korean, and Japanese lacquerware, which has long been noted to cause dermatitis. The lacquer tree and America's poison ivies are kin, as too are mangoes, pistachios, and cashews, all being members of the Anacardiaceae family of plants, and all of which can cause allergic reactions in sensitive people.

Given what even the least woodsy of us knows, you wouldn't think that anyone would deliberately eat poison ivy. But some do, though fortunately in small quantities. Out west, where poison oak is widespread, they sell poison-oak honey, which hurts no one. Some people even eat it in the belief that it will give them immunity to urushiol, although there is little scientific evidence for this theory. Homeopathic medicine believes that "'like cures like" so that people suffering physical symptoms similar to those caused by poison ivy can be cured by taking a tincture of poison ivy that has been so diluted you literally can't detect any urushiol in the solution. The cure, called *Rhus toxicodendron* or *Rhus tox.*, or simply poison ivy, has been used for typhoid fever, swollen glands, sore muscles, back pain, dermatological complaints (including measles, chicken pox, herpes, and hives), the flu, sore throats, carpal tunnel, arthritis, rheumatism, and—of course—poison-ivy infection itself.

The remarkable discovery of the curative powers of urushiol was made by an eighteenth-century French army surgeon, Dr. Dufresnoy, when a student suffering from severe eczema accidentally ate some poison ivy and cured himself. Dufresnoy tried on himself the effect of drinking an infusion of twelve leaves, which upset his stomach and made him sweat and pee. He later found poison ivy helped paralytics. English doctor I. Alderson's 1794 treatise introduced the poison ivy cure to the English-speaking world. Paralytic patients treated with poison ivy reported that feeling and mobility returned to their limbs. The cure, in pill or liquid form, is readily available online if you care to try it. Or you can make your own, as Dufresnoy did, by picking some poison ivy leaves and brewing a tea. One homeopathic site observes that the active ingredient, toxicodendric acid, is "most potent" at night, in bad weather, and during the summer, so you might wait for an warm evening thunderstorm to do your gathering.

Should you forget to wear gloves when harvesting your leaves, you can always try one of any number of more orthodox remedies for poison-ivy poisoning. During World War II, the U.S. Army injected soldiers suffering from poison ivy with a green solution of poison-ivy leaves soaked in alcohol that *Time Magazine* claimed ended the itching in two hours and the rash in five days. It never caught on in civilian circles. Most of us probably remember painting our arms and legs with garishly pink calamine lotion when cursed with poison ivy. Calamine is a mixture of zinc and iron oxides named after "La Calamine," a Belgian town home to a zinc mine. Since the U.S. Food and Drug Administration has declared calamine lotion utterly ineffective in alleviating rashes and itching, you might try Ivy Block, developed for the U.S. Forest Service after it tired of losing thousands of man hours to poison-ivy infections. Ivy Block uses bentonite clay to bind with urushiol and so prevent its reaching the skin. Bentonite is also used in antiperspirants and cat litter, both of which may be lying around your house as potential homemade sources of poison-ivy itch cure. Another intriguing product is Tecnu's Oak-n-Ivy, which uses solvents to wash the urushiol off your skin. Tecnu's first skin cleanser was designed to wash radioactive dust off those of us who survived a nuclear attack; only later did someone find a more immediate use for it. The cheapest cure is to rub yourself with jewelweed (*Impatiens capensis* and *I. pallida*), juicy-stemmed wildflowers often found growing near poison ivy, though many experts consider their curative powers exaggerated.

You could go to a doctor, but to receive effective treatment you'd have to know what infected you, and here too you'd have a problem. Most botanists recognize four species of poison oak and ivy in North America, Pacific poison oak (*Toxicodendron diversilobum*), Atlantic poison oak (*Toxicodendron pubescens*), eastern poison ivy (*Toxicodendron radicans*), and western poison ivy (*Toxicodendron rydbergii*), and a fifth cousin, poison sumac (*Toxicodendron vernix*). But there are at least six subspecies of poison ivy scattered throughout North America. We're in better shape than east Asia, which is cursed with some sixteen different kinds of *Toxicodendron*. And just to confuse things, it's only been forty years since science called the poison ivy in my backyard *Toxicodendron radicans;* before then, it was *Rhus radicans,* Linnaeus having lumped the poison ivies, oaks, and sumacs together with the nonpoisonous sumacs, whose Greek name was *Rhus. Toxicodendron* means poison-leaved, an entirely appropriate name. The two genuses are closely related and, in the case of poison sumac, even their leaves look alike. But the *Rhus* have red berries while the *Toxicodendron* have white. And of course the latter make you itch.

Not even the saying "leaflets three, let it be" is entirely accurate. Poison sumac has many more leaflets than three, and poison ivy can have as many as five. The number three, in any case, would eliminate the boxelder (*Acer negundo*), which, when young, really is nearly indistinguishable from poison ivy; Virginia creeper (*Parthenocissus quinquefolia*), which usually has five leaves but sometimes only three and often lives in the same tree as poison ivy; kudzu (*Pueraria lobata*), which also has three leaves and climbs trees but which only the truly ignorant could confuse with poison ivy; blackberries and raspberries, which often have groups of three leaflets but also have spines, which poison ivy never does; and strawberries, which are three-leaved. Such confusion must make one happy that the *Toxicodendrons* aren't native to Ireland: Saint Patrick would have been hard-pressed to use poison ivy to explain the Trinity.

SASSAFRAS

Springtime is tea time, when I travel back fifty years and across two states to walk behind my father into the woods in search of sassafras. Then I needed no greater proof of his omniscience than his unfailing ability to lead me and my siblings to a sassafras thicket. That, grown, I know every nearly fencerow in eastern America harbors such thickets decreases my father's woodlore not a whit—nor my delight when first scenting sassafras roots red with spring sap after a winter of commercial teas. And that the government would have me believe my father's tonic cancer-causing but strengthens my belief that these are lesser days than yore. Who would not tempt fate to walk once again with the giants of his youth?

Nor am I the only child to have fallen under the spell of sassafras. English Romantic essayist Charles Lamb declared in 1822, "This wood boiled down to a kind of tea, and tempered with an infusion of milk and sugar, hath to some tastes a delicacy beyond the China luxury." Known as saloop, sassafras tea was, according to Lamb, the favorite beverage of young chimney sweeps, costing but three halfpennies. And when even this sum was beyond their means, "being penniless, they will yet hang their black heads over the ascending steam, to gratify one sense if possible."

Just as my father's spring tonic might have carried with it the seeds of cancer, so too Lamb's saloop was more than a poor boy's delight. Saloop originally was salep, a beverage made from the flour of ground orchid bulbs. And salep comes from the Arabic for "fox testicles," a reference to the bulbs' shape, *orchid* itself coming from the Greek word for testicle. Drinks made from orchid roots were long thought to be aphrodisiacs. Up until the last century, saloop was a popular drink in both England and Germany, as well as the Middle East. Salep is still so popular an ingredient in Turkish ice cream that conservationists fear the orchids whose roots are used may be extirpated.

Salep consumption may date back to ancient times, but sassafras is a New World tree, growing throughout the eastern United States into the Plains. That it came to be associated with Turkish aphrodisiacs is in no small part thanks to Spanish physician Nicholas Monardes, whose 1574 Spanish text, translated into English as *Joyfull Newes Out of the Newe Founde Worlde,* included an enthusiastic endorsement of sassafras as a cure for nearly everything that ailed you, from plague to syphilis. Monardes got his information from Spanish explorers, who got theirs from French Huguenots they had tortured in Florida. These unfortunate Frenchmen had advised the Spanish suffering from fevers thought to be caused by miasmas and unclean water to imbibe a tea of what they called sassafras—probably a mispronunciation of saxifrage. So fragrant were the sassafras trees that the Spaniards thought them the cinnamon of the East Indies. Monardes writes, "The tree and bowes are very light, the rinde being tasted, hath an excellent sweete smell, and it is somewhat like to the smell of Fenell, with muche sweetenesse of taste, and of pleasaunt smell insomuch that a little quantity of this Wood being in a chamber, filleth the ayre contained in it."

Monardes began a short-lived sassafras craze, with English merchants seeking their fortunes in sassafras, which was worth its weight in gold. Thomas Hariot declared the tree a remedy for "the French Poxe, ... the Plague, and many other Maladies." Sir Walter Raleigh obtained a sassafras monopoly from Queen Elizabeth I, selling the stuff for one- to two-thousand pounds a ton, with 1,000-percent profits. Bristol merchants subsidized voyages to the New World to collect sassafras, and colonists in Jamestown, Virginia, were ordered to produce a hundred pounds of it per person. That sassafras, in fact, cured nothing eventually brought prices down, ending the craze, but not before those who drank it were embarrassed by its multiple uses. Peter Kalm heard in 1748 that "Some *Englishmen* related, that some years ago it had been customary in *London* to drink a kind of tea of the flowers of sassafras, because it was looked upon as very salutary; but upon recollecting that the same potion was much used against the venereal disease, it was soon left off, lest those that used it, should be looked upon as infected with that disease." Seventy-four years later, Londoners were still drinking sassafras tea, according to Lamb.

Sassafras flavored numerous nineteenth-century concoctions for blood purifiers and thinners, rheumatic liniment, cod-liver oil, blood and kidney tea, eye salve, diarrhea, toothache, beer, wine, and the incredibly popular Godfrey's Cordial, a potent mix of sassafras, caraway, coriander, aniseed, water, molasses, and opium, "universally approved of for the cholick, and all Manner of pains in the bowels fluxes, fevers, small-pox, measles, rheumatism, coughs, colds, and restlessness in Men, Women, and Children, and Particularly for several Ailments incident to Child-bearing Woman, and Relief of young Children in bearing their Teeth," according to Dr. Benjamin Godfrey himself, who also advertised that it "is Sold in most Cities, Boroughs, and Market-Towns throughout Great-Britain and Ireland, and in most publick Streets in London." Ten gallons of Godfrey's Cordial were sold every week in Coventry, England, alone, enough for twelve thousand doses, three thousand of which went to babies less than two years old. This statistic may help explain Lamb's chimney sweepers' love of saloop, flavored with what young boys had been taking since infancy.

But these concoctions were anything but health-giving, according to the U.S. Food and Drug Administration, which determined that safrole, a volatile oil found in sassafras, causes liver cancer in lab rats and so banned it fifty years ago. One source estimates that a single cup of sassafras tea contains five times the amount of safrole thought to be hazardous to humans. While you can now buy safrole-free sassafras extract in the grocery store, sassafras lovers claim it's inferior to the real thing. And they like to point out that foods like basil, pepper, cocoa, mace, nutmeg, and parsley also contain safrole, but we still eat them.

But safrole isn't just a carcinogen. My childhood tea's flavoring turns out to be a main ingredient in the manufacture of MDMA, methylenedioxymethamphetamine, or ecstasy.

First synthesized in the early twentieth century, the drug was largely ignored until the 1960s, when it began to be used by doctors to treat psychiatric patients and by recreational drug users. It is now one of the more common illegal drugs, popular because it promotes feelings of euphoria and empathy. Which the tea certainly does for me. So I have taken my son, Edward, with me to look for sassafras.

Dangerous or not, drinking sassafras tea in the spring is a Leland tradition that must be handed down. Edward and I go, hand in hand, up House Mountain, escorted by my father's ghost, peering at fence rows and woods' edges. Finding a thicket, we set to work pulling up smaller sprouts until we have enough root stock to make a pot of tea.

These saplings are often clones joined at the root. Roots more thick than those of sassafras tie my son to me and me to my father, and he to his father, and he to his, and so on through generations back to the Indians who invented steeping the roots in water. Sassafras tea inhibits seeds other than sassafras from germinating, and researchers think the tree may build its thickets by poisoning competitors. What I teach my son might just poison him in ways undreamt of by the FDA.

Sassafras's roots stretch deep into the past. American sassafras (*Sassafras albidum*) has two close cousins in Asia, Chinese sassafras (*S. tzumu*) and Taiwanese sassafras (*S. randaiense*). These disjunct relatives, separated from their American cousin by thousands of miles, suggest sassafras was widely distributed. What we think of as American trees—sassafras, hickory, magnolia, tulip poplar—have kin in China, and I have met Asian students who felt at home walking through what I had hitherto thought of as American woods. So too my son and I hike different forests when we climb House Mountain, he scuffing leaves in a Virginia wood and I struggling to keep up with my father in a coastal Carolina thicket gone these fifty years.

☙ BRIAR PATCH

Midsummer, and I'm cursing the thorns that Celia's blackberries have sprouted to keep me from their fruit. Ouch, ouch, and double ouch. They snag and tear at me as if malevolently alive—which I suppose they are, since they're part of a plant, after all. Not that I'm supposed to think that intention governs the actions of blackberry thorns.

But why are they here at all? Not to stop me or Celia or any of our kind. Blackberries are far older residents of North America than we newcomer humans, so their defenses evolved against predators other than ourselves. And those were probably after the plants themselves, not the fruit. Deer and rabbits, for example, love blackberry leaves, and I have often followed deer paths into a blackberry thicket in order to reach the fruit. But even the toughest deer's mouth must learn to avoid the nasty thorns that adorn the canes. The ripe fruit, of course, attract dozens of predators, from birds such as quail, turkey, blackbirds, bluebirds, mockingbirds, robins, and redbirds, to mammals such as the deer who also nibble the leaves, possums, foxes, raccoons, squirrels, mice, and bear.

Darwin and company explain thorns by way of natural selection, Darwin writing in an 1868 letter, "That Natural Selection would tend to produce the most formidable thorns will be admitted by every one who has observed the distribution in South America and Africa (*vide* Livingstone) of thorn-bearing plants, for they always appear where the bushes grow isolated and are exposed to the attacks of mammals. Even in England it has been noticed that all spine-bearing and sting-bearing plants are palatable to quadrupeds, when the thorns are crushed." Fellow theorist Alfred Russel Wallace cited the paucity of both thorny plants and herbivores on oceanic islands as support for the theory that thorns were vegetable defenses. And that the nearly thornless smooth blackberry (*Rubus Canadensis*) grows at higher elevations in Virginia where, presumably, there was less herbivore pressure explains to some its lack of thorns.

But not all scientists immediately accepted natural selection as a valid explanation for vegetable defenses. English botanist and theologian George Henslow proposed "The Origin of Plant-Structures by Self-Adaptation to the Environment, exemplified by Desert or Xerophilous Plants," arguing that *"form is a result of habit,"* that the environment produces physical changes in plants which, if kept long enough, become heritable. Thus, a lack of water caused leaves to roll up and become spinelike, and, if prolonged, this spiny nature will be passed on to future plants. Such heritable characteristics were reversible by improving conditions: add water, and the spines vanish.

So associated with the idea of the heritability of acquired characteristics is early nineteenth-century French scientist Jean-Baptiste Lamarck that the concept is named Lamarckism after him. Lamarck famously assumed that giraffes stretching their necks to reach leaves on higher branches would acquire longer necks that they would in turn pass on to their offspring, much as if a track athlete could pass her leg muscles to her children. Darwin's idea that longer-necked giraffes produced more offspring than did the shorter-necked is what we believe today.

Differ though they might, all these theorists were scientists, quarreling, not over evolution, but over the mechanisms that governed evolution. Not so the religious, who turned to Genesis's explanation: "cursed is the ground for thy sake; in sorrow shalt thou eat of it all the days of thy life; Thorns also and thistles shall it bring forth to thee." Today, Kentucky's Creation Museum depicts a prelapsarian Garden of Eden where the plants are thornless and the animals vegetarian, carnivores and thorns appearing after the Fall, the museum claims; their Web site explains, "There is evidence that thorns are formed from altered leaves."

So thorns are, to some of the religious, a product of the Fall. My students and I debate this endlessly: from whence come the thorns and thistles with which we torment those closest to us? God? The Devil? Nature? Nurture? Are we born innocent or fallen? Mondays I'm comforted by Christ's observation regarding children that "of such is the kingdom of God": that we're basically decent and the thorns learned and Lamarckian; Tuesdays a *Lord of the Flies* cynicism about what we've all seen on children's playgrounds makes me suspect neither I nor Jesus fully appreciates the innate depravity of mankind.

The all too physical thorns borne by Celia's blackberries tear but our flesh. Would that the spines we grow were as easily removed, our prickly personalities the results of years of behaviors carefully cultivated to keep the world at bay. We've all hidden behind barriers thorny enough to rival Sleeping Beauty's, and hung though they be with the corpses of those who tried to get close to us, who among us will take a chainsaw to such successful defenses? We may curse the blackberry's canes, but far sharper are the briars we whip each other with when angry or threatened.

Most of my thorns are my very own growths, the warped weirdness of half a century of misadventures with my fellow humans: Acquired characteristics, one might say, and all too inheritable. Surely you've noticed your child perfectly copying your vices, parroting your curses, bristling over the same silly slights you bristle over, torturing family members with the same exquisite tortures you've practiced all these years. Edward begins to be my son in ways lamentable, in ways that I prove myself all too much my father's son, and in ways my father no doubt proved himself his father's son, and he his and he his, and on and on and on, son following in father's thorny footsteps, perhaps as far back as Adam, but each perfectly adapted to the peculiar conditions of our individual nuclear family's radioactive relations. One might write a treatise on the speciation of metaphysical thorns, how the multitudinous offspring of the last common ancestral thorn hied themselves to our great-great-great-great-great grandparents' families and, like tortoises isolated on the islands of the Galapagos, grew so different one from the other that those wise in the ways of accursed families can tell from whose a particular thorny personality issues: why you and your Uncle Vernon are such pains in the ass in the selfsame way, why my ex-wife and her siblings share the same lamentable personality defects, and why I and my siblings invariably offend each other and the world in the same sad ways.

Brambles bear berries as well as thorns, and the former are what lead us to tear our flesh in summer fields so that, come winter, we can remember warmth a possibility. But try getting Edward to put more berries in his bucket than in his mouth. After half an hour's berry picking, my bucket's getting full, but Edward's has only half a dozen berries, his mouth and hands are stained purple, and, his stomach full, he's ready to quit. Useless the talk of jam in January; what child in summer thinks winter will return? Only aging parents, for whom each new summer seems shorter, each winter longer than the last, are willing to defer for months the pleasure of summer's berries—and even we are known to sneak a snack when no one's looking. Come January, though, both Edward and I smear too much jam upon our toast and, for a breakfast moment, remember the sun upon our backs and berries in our mouths, forgetting, for the moment, the thorns.

HEDGES

Stone walls grow only where stone was so plentiful as to require moving. But almost all settlers needed something to wall out intrusive people and animals. The cheaper and less troublesome something, the better. So many turned to hedges as leafy barriers to trespass. Just which plants best served as hedge material was contentious, favored plants commanding high prices until edged out by a new miracle vegetable, many of which escaped cultivation and still linger in valley fields and forests.

Virginians favor boxwood hedges, and not just any box: English box is denser and fuller than its leggier, more open American cousin. Those who know can sort the two kinds by their leaves, the American being lankier than the rounder English, the plants apparently intent on representing their respective national characters. I learned this distinction by marrying a Virginian who could walk a Lexington street and tell at a glance whether or not the hedge we passed passed social muster. I learned the difference, too late to save our marriage, but, to those even less in the know than I, I pass as an expert on the difference between a fat John Bull and a lean Uncle Sam of a hedge.

Not that the distinction's worth the making: American boxwood's a misnomer. Both it and English boxwood not only hale from Europe, they're close kin, being but cultivars of the same species, *Buxus sempevirens,* a plant native to Europe and North Africa. And, sssh, I'll whisper this so unsuspecting Virginians won't overhear, another name for both is *common* boxwood. English box may be the more compact of the two, reaching a height of three to five feet and often kept by trimming to only inches high, while the so-called American box can grow twenty feet high. To complicate matters, there really are American boxwoods, but they grow in the Caribbean and South America, not the middle Atlantic states. And even if you could grow it as far north as Virginia, Puerto Rico box just hasn't the cachet of English box.

While genteel Virginians may have enjoyed perambulating their boxwood gardens, they didn't enjoy it nearly as much as their descendants think they did. Historians credit master gardener Arthur Shurcliff with popularizing boxwood. When designing Williamsburg, Virginia's gardens in the 1930s, Shurcliff fell in love with boxwood and used, and overused, it everywhere, imparting to his reconstructed village a formality and gentility its ancestor never possessed. Status-conscious Virginians ignore or never knew that Shurcliff based his gardens not on Tidewater designs but on those of colonial North Carolina, a region some Virginians have long looked askance at, colonial planter William Byrd calling his southern neighbor, "Lubberland." Byrd's famous James River plantation, Westover, has old boxwoods large enough to be, ahem, American. To rub it in even further, some botanists question English boxwood's right to be called English, thinking it may have been brought to the islands by the Romans.

Boxwood's appeal is that it loves to be clipped into formal hedges and bizarre topiaries. Enterprising gardeners are said to have clipped valley hedges for free, taking the cuttings and sticking them in river sandbars and banks, where they rapidly put out roots and, provided they weren't washed away in floods, provided plants to sell to aspiring gentry. English boxwood's compact nature lent itself much more to these practices than did American boxwood. Thus, minuscule hedges, which seem but months old, may prove decades older than their taller neighbors, whose ragged appearances makes them seem senescent. My uncle had such shin-high hedges of box lining the paths of his formal garden. When he died, the people who bought his place uprooted a two-hundred-year-old garden and planted grass instead.

Not that uprooting boxwoods is an easy job. When Celia decided her fifteen-year-old hedge of English box had to go, we thought a morning would suffice. By noon, however, we'd managed to remove but one plant, and that only after hooking a chain around its roots and dragging it out with a pickup. Long after those who planted them have themselves been planted and forgotten, boxwoods live on, as in Sehorn Hollow on House Mountain's flank. There, on a slight rise looking west toward North Mountain, the house burned so long ago both chimney and cellar have disappeared. Tree-sized and ragged, the boxes alone remain, giving a vague sense of where gardens once stood. Adventitious shoots, so old they seem at first hedges run wild, reach each year farther up and down the road, spreading their genteel vision of America.

As befits a genteel vegetable, boxwood is never invasive. Not so its faux look-alike, privet, which is what I grew up with, my parents having walled in our family clothesline with a hedge of privet. Easy to grow, easy to trim, privet is the arriviste's reply to the slower-growing boxwood's aristocratic hauteur. Young, I knew neither that the hedge should have been box nor that the clothesline should have been an indoor drier so that passersby would not glimpse our ragged underwear through the privet's less dense branches. My son's more fortunate; having read

Harry Potter, he knows that Harry's muggle relatives, the Dursleys, betray their decidedly low social status by living on Privet Drive.

Not that privet is universally reviled. Colonial gardeners John Bartram of Philadelphia and Henry Prince of New York both sold it in their mail-order catalogs, Prince explaining, "it is only their being common which causes them to be less often used." Too hot and humid for boxwoods, the Deep South relied instead privet, which had long been used for hedges and topiary in Europe, where it is native. When putting on the dog, privet calls itself Ligustrum, after the fancy moniker Linnaeus gave it, *Ligustrum vulgare*. *Vulgare* is Latin for *common*, which Prince had called the plant, though others are content to term it *vulgar*. *Ligustrum* is what the Romans are said to have called privet. While Lexington's more prestigious streets boast stately homes with boxwood hedges worthy of playing hide-and-seek in, were one willing to trespass, my less prestigious neighborhood favors privet, which some people shave as close as a military haircut and others let grow as long as a ponytail. By any name, privet's numerous, small, white flowers laden the early summer air with the thick scent of childhood, and a walk begun on Massie Street concludes with me five hundred miles away, hanging clothes in South Carolina, while the bees hum in the hedge.

The scruffier woods around Lexington, filled with many an exotic species, often have privet in them. So common an escapee was it in 1800 that French naturalist André Michaux thought it native. Naturalized in many states today are Amur privet, border privet, California privet, Chinese privet, European privet, glossy privet, Japanese privet, Sri Lanka privet, Tschonosky privet, and waxyleaf privet. The Southeast is especially plagued, and many states have declared privets invasive or obnoxious. Mature plants produce hundreds of small black fruits that are favorites of birds and small mammals and boys with peashooters, who spread them everywhere. Extensive thickets are nearly impossible to eradicate, and getting rid of even a single privet can be daunting; one that comes out from beneath the sidewalk beside my house I have cut back to the root for years, but each spring it sends up new shoots. That following a neighbor's advice I myself planted it years ago as a cutting merely adds to the insult.

I'm trying to uproot my privet because I've decided to gentrify my yard with a rose hedge, whose floral beauty and thorny impassibility made them farming favorites for centuries, with the result that nearly every state is plagued with thickets of thorn. Michaux noticed the Cherokee rose (*Rosa laevigata*) growing wild in Georgia about 1800 and thought it native. The plant actually hails from China south through Vietnam and was introduced here sometime in the eighteenth century. Popular legend, however, has it that the flower is native, claiming it sprang from tears shed by Cherokee mothers on the infamous Trail of Tears, when President Andrew Jackson forcibly removed the indigenous Indians from the eastern states. In 1916 the Georgia state legislature, reasoning "whereas, The Cherokee Rose, having its origin among the aborigines of the northern portion of the State of Georgia, is indigenous to its soil, and grows with equal luxuriance in every county of the State," declared it their state flower. British author Gavin Menzies claimed recently, in *1421: The Year China Discovered the World*, that Chinese sailors brought the Cherokee rose in flower pots to America during their hitherto unreported travels about the globe.

But the rose that ate the Shenandoah Valley is the *Rosa multiflora*, perhaps the most reviled of hedge roses, because it is the hardiest and hence widest spread, its roots reaching north into Canada and throughout the United States with the exception of the Great Basin, the high plains, and the southeastern coastal plain. The species name, *multiflora*, refers to the multitude of small white or pink flowers borne in bundles, so numerous that single plants can produce five hundred thousand seeds a year, each of which can remain viable for up to twenty years. Birds love them, which makes you wonder what one wildlife expert was thinking when he wrote, "It does not spread objectionably," or what two others were contemplating in 1949 when they wrote their eight-page *Multiflora Rose for Living Fences and Wildlife Cover.*

Swedish botanist Carl Peter Thunberg was the first European to describe the multiflora, which he found growing in a Japanese garden in 1775. The Japanese appear to have imported it from Korea. It was growing in a New York botanical garden in 1811, and during the nineteenth century was widely used as an ornamental and later as rootstock for grafted roses. So common was it that Harriet Beecher Stowe thought it American, writing that the front of Uncle Tom's Cabin was "covered by a large scarlet bignonia and a native multiflora rose, which, entwisting and interlacing, left scarce a vestige of the rough logs to be seen." Ironically it's the bignonia or crossvine that's native, and the multiflora that's not. The U.S. Soil and Conservation Service planted it in the 1930s to curb erosion, while nurseries sold it for hedges and highway plantings, and others sang its potential as a food and cover crop. With such government support, multiflora spread and spread and spread.

In Virginia's valley, it's everywhere: conscientious farmers, listening to their extension agents' promises of a hedge thick enough in three years to stop everything but chickens, planted it at one foot intervals along the edges of their fields. Chickens' winged relatives soon spread the rose hips into neighboring fields and forests, where they grew into thorny tangles ten feet high and thick. On slow winter Saturdays, I used to take my handsaw and clippers and walk my fields and woods, cutting off at the ground arching canes whose thorns have been said to flatten tractor tires. But summer mornings, when a million multiflora flowers bloomed, I'd regret—for a moment—my labor, and revel in perfume thick enough to spread like honey. I lost those rose-hedged fields when I lost my English boxwoods and my Virginia wife, all of which grow, well, rosier with time, so I've decided to eradicate my privet and plant multiflora roses along my city fence. In a few years, I'll be ten years younger and happier when I smell again a Shenandoah summer.

VEGETABLE ARMATURE

Vegetable armature, they call it, the thorns and spines and prickles that plants bear to our annoyance. While blackberries might explain the fundamentals of such armatures, there are trees in our woods so over-armed that scientists can only speculate as to what drove them to such distraction.

Take the honey locust (*Gleditsia triacanthos*). You're most likely to run into a tame variety on a street or in a park, where it's planted because of its fast growth, blow-away leaves, and dappled shade. My college has two nice-sized ones outside its administration building. In the spring, five-inch-long racemes of creamy-white flowers seduce the passersby with their delicious perfume. Come fall, the perfume turns into seed pods filled with an edible, honey-sweet green goo you can dig out with finger or tooth and in which float the seeds. All in all, a lovely tree.

But a quarter mile away, along Woods Creek Trail, hiding behind a sycamore, stands a wild honey locust, offspring perhaps of those nearby collegiate trees, since the tree's native range is the Mississippi and Ohio River valleys. Surrounded by rival trees, this one's grown tall and straight, unlike its college-pampered, open-spaced relatives. But what draws your attention to this otherwise unremarkable tree are the bouquets of spines scattered along its trunk and branches, each clump with ten to twenty vicious, branching spines, some more than a foot long, each tip ever so much sharper than you'd think, and all intertwined one with the other so, try to grab one, and a dozen poke you. Profligate of pain, the honey locust grows spines everywhere, singles sticking out from branches and bundles from the trunk. Wanting a spine to grace my mantle to remind me of Mother Nature's nature, I suffered a dozen pokes and prods grabbing one. Finding it twisted easily, I thought removing it but a moment's work but took five minutes to twist it loose.

What horrible animal did the ancestral honey locust deter with such Pentagon overkill? Nobody knows. Whatever it was, it's no longer around. The pods fall to the ground, where they're eaten by gray and fox squirrels, white-tailed deer, quail and crows, and possums, as well as cattle and hogs, none of which needs to brave thorns to get to the fruit, although many a human has rued the day he or she walked barefoot under a honey locust. Older trees cease producing thorns in their crowns, so that the upper reaches of the tree are often thornless. Whatever beast drove the tree to defend itself with such extravagance must, then, have been after lower leaves and branches, if not the trunk itself. Think elephant.

Which is what Daniel Janzen thought when musing on the evolution of large fruit-bearing trees, like the avocado, in the jungles of Central America. Might not, he wondered, have now-extinct Pleiostocene megafauna such as mastadons and giant sloths guided these trees' evolution? Others applied Janzen's idea to big-seeded, large-thorned North America trees like the honey locust. If indeed giant browsers drove the evolution of spines, they did so on more than one continent, because *Gleditsia* grows in both Americas and in Asia. All twelve species sport thorns, and Swedish botanist Carl Peter Thunberg thought the Japanese version so fearsome he named it *horrid*.

Janzen was not the first to take an interest in America's megafauna. Two hundred years earlier, Thomas Jefferson had cited mammoth remains to refute assertions of American inferiority made by French naturalist Georges-Louis Leclerc, Comte de Buffon: "To whatever animal we ascribe these remains, it is certain such a one has existed in America, and that it has been the largest of all terrestrial beings. It should have sufficed to have rescued the earth it inhabited, and the atmosphere it breathed, from the imputation of impotence in the conception and nourishment of animal life on a large scale: to have stifled, in its birth, the opinion of a writer [Buffon], the most learned too of all others in the science of animal history, that in the new world, `La nature vivante est beaucoup moins agissante, beaucoup moins forte:' that nature is less active, less energetic on one side of the globe than she is on the other." Jefferson's preoccupation with mega-faunal remains led critics to dub him "Mr. Mammoth" and advise, "Go, wretch resign thy presidential chair, / Disclose thy secret measures, foul and fair, / Go search with curious eye, for horned frogs, / Mid the Wild Louisianian bogs: / Or, where the Ohio rolls his turbid stream, / Dig for huge bones, thy glory and scheme." Artist and naturalist Charles Willson Peale famously displayed an eleven-foot-high, seventeen-foot-long mammoth (what today we call a mastodon) in his popular Philadelphia museum and helped arrange the bones of a giant sloth, later named *Megalonyx jeffersoni* after Jefferson. Jefferson thought such monsters to still live, writing in *Notes on the State of Virginia* that "The bones of the Mammoth, which have been found in America, are as large as those found in the old world. It may be asked, why I insert the Mammoth, as if it still existed? I ask in return, why I should omit it, as if it did not exist? Such is the oeconomy of nature, that no instance can be produced of her having permitted any one race of her animals to become extinct; of her having formed any link in her great work so weak as to be broken. To add to this, the traditionary testimony of the Indians, that this animal still exists in the northern and western parts of America, would be adding the light of a taper to that of the meridian sun." And he asked Lewis and Clark to keep an eye out for them in their expedition to the Pacific.

Honey locust is merely the most fearsome of America's armored trees. The black locust (*Robinia pseudoacacia*), which looks similar to the honey but is not as closely related as previously thought, lacks the other's fearsome spines, sporting instead pairs of short thorns at the base of its leaves. Not that these thorns aren't effective; try reaching into a thicket of black locusts and you'll understand their deterrent power, since they grow on every branch, stem, and trunk of young locusts. Deer and cattle confine their dining to young plants. The older trees know this, gradually ceasing to produce thorns on older wood, since nothing eats them past ten years old. Black locust, then, unlike honey locust, either didn't get carried away with its defense budget or didn't face the same grazing pressure that honey locust did. Since black locust's bean pods are dessicated things scarcely worth the time to look at, much less eat, I suppose plant eaters went after the sweeter, juicier honey locust, which is merely a plant version of honey drawing more flies and herbivores than vinegar.

When he was younger, Edward and I picked the thorns off the younger locusts and licked and applied them to our foreheads, becoming rhinoceri. He is much too sage to play such silly games now, but, in a fit of nostalgia for his fast-passing childhood, I will sometimes transmogrify myself when no one else is around and snort and chase my shadow down the road. Every so often, when reaching for a thorn, I'm surprised to see it move and discover a locust treehopper, a small, hunchbacked bug which looks very much like a thorn. Since lots of treehoppers have learned to play rhinoceros, and at least two of these play on locust trees, I cannot tell the species. No matter; although we've never been properly introduced, the bug and I both know the power of camouflage, it avoiding predators by looking thornlike and I dodging dull adulthood for as long as it takes a thorn to fall from off my forehead.

Would that all armor were as temporary. But many of us are hid behind so thick a screen of thorns and spines and bristles that no charming princess or prince charming could ever hack through to wake our sleeping souls. My soul shriveling, I take me to a field gone wild out Old Farm Road to see what will become of me should I not change my ways. There, grapefruit-sized, wizened brains of—take your pick—aliens, monkeys, or mean old men rot upon the branches where someone or something has impaled them. Or so Edward believed after he and I first visited the marvel which is the Osage orange or bodark tree (*Maclura pomifera*). The wrinkled fruit hang from thorn-laden branches from autumn late into winter, falling one by one to the ground where they lie, untouched, uneaten, turning yellow, then brown, as they slowly dissolve into a mushy mess. Cut them, and they ooze bitter-tasting white liquid that blackens like dried blood and causes a rash wherever it touches you. Only a God troubled by nightmares could have dreamed such a tree.

Maclura pomifera hails from the Red River Valley of Oklahoma and Texas, though it has traveled worldwide since its discovery by the French, who called it *bois d'arc*, after the Indians' use of it for bows. We Americans corrupted that to bodark and decided the tree, which sports inch-long thorns along its trunks and branches, would make a hedge, as proverb has it, "horse high, bull strong, and hog tight." A *Maclura* craze ensued as the Plains were settled following the Civil War, the fruit became a commodity on the Chicago Board of Trade, a Kansas nursery advertised for sale one hundred thousand trees, and some people estimate sixty thousand miles of monkey brain trees lined Midwestern fields—until barbed wire ruined things.

By then, someone had brought the Osage orange to Rockbridge County. It may have been Patrick Henry, because his plantation, Red Hill, east over the Blue Ridge, has what many think the world's oldest Osage orange tree, a twenty-six-foot-plus round giant whose hollow trunk means no one can count its rings and tell how old it really is. Whoever brought them, monkey brains have scattered themselves throughout Virginia, so that you're never far from one. They're mostly wild, few people willing to put up with brains littering their lawns.

Few animals bother with them either, mostly squirrels that pick at them, leaving the remains beneath the tree they fell from. What animal, some people wonder, grew tall enough and mean enough to reach ripe monkey brains and carry them away? Whatever it was, they think, the tree grew thorns to stop it from eating the monkey brains' leaves and tearing its branches off. But no such behemoth stalked the Red River Valley any time in the near past. Enter the Pleistocene megafauna again, the same animals said to have encouraged the honey locust to grow hornery. Perhaps these vanished mammals, with mouths large enough to swallow grapefruit-sized balls, also nibbled monkey brains. Now extinct, they are remembered—perhaps with sadness—only by the thorny-branched trees lined with rotting brains. The trees may be sad because some think the Indians killed off the giant sloths and mastodons that ate the monkey brains' yearly offering with bows made of Osage orange.

Among the trees that remember, if but genetically, their close encounters with giant sloths and mastodons is the angry devil's walking stick (*Aralia spinosa*). Native to much of the eastern United States, this small tree gets it name from its trunk, which is so thick with prickles that none but the devil could grasp it. While thorns are the children of stems and spines of leaves, prickles are overgrown children of bark. Devotee of disturbed sites, the devil's walking stick, also known as Hercules' club and prickly ash, shoots up as a branchless, prickle-covered stick for the first few years before branching out, with a pit-bull collar of toothed prickles lining the leaf scars. During its early years you should cut it down and keep it behind your front door so that, when people wax sentimental over Mother Nature, you can whack them back to reality. Whatever grazed this thorny nightmare was no Bambi, for whitetail deer turn their noses up at *Aralia*. Once again, vanished herbivores are invoked to explain this devilish tree. Perhaps elk and bison grazed upon thickets of young walking sticks before the Europeans exterminated the herds. Perhaps the giant sloths and mastodons of the Pleistocene delighted in the clusters of purple berries calling attention to themselves on red stems set against the light green of what are the largest leaves in North America. You can't grasp their size by looking at what appear to be inches-long leaves. But these are leaflets, parts of a larger leaf, which often branches two or three times so that the whole leaf comprises dozens of leaflets covering six square feet of air. And maybe those slightly toxic berries evolved their bright colors to call in birds that feast upon them to this day. Who knows?

Sometimes confused with the devil's walking stick, with which it shares the popular names Hercules' club and prickly ash, is the toothache tree (*Zanthoxylum clava-herculis*). Found primarily in the coastal plain south of Virginia, the toothache tree, like the devil's walking stick, has a trunk littered with thorns. To its armament, however, the toothache tree has added gum-numbing leaves, whence its popular name. As a child, I used to numb my mouth nibbling on these citrusy-smelling, bitter leaves as I walked the back dunes of the barrier islands. One toothache tree grew on the very tip of Porcher's Bluff where my sister Cheves lived, and Christmases when I visited her, I'd numb my way back to a childhood as long gone as those half-mythical megafauna invoked by this and that expert to explain these now overarmed plants. As the toothache tree ages, though, it too grows kinder, gentler, covering its thorns in cork, childproofing its once lethal trunk. Nothing but wandering children and the larvae of the giant swallowtail butterfly (*Papilio cresphontes*) eat the tree's leaves today. This caterpillar, called an orange dog and looking like wet bird shit, is hated by Florida's citrus growers, since the toothache tree and orange are relatives enough for both to be good eating. But the butterfly itself ranges as far north as Canada and west to the Rockies, happily feeding on the toothache tree far from orange and grapefruit groves.

Trees so needlessly overarmed remind me of my own bellicose species. I know a man who doesn't hunt who nevertheless owns twenty guns and rifles, and many a man and woman drives armed to work in Lexington, Virginia, of all places. I teach at a school with an armory for its students, live in a nation that murders seventeen thousand of its own citizens each year, sells thirty-seven thousand firearms yearly, and hoards nearly ten thousand nuclear warheads. I myself have shotgun, pistol, and baseball bat at hand. Any child's playground will soon teach you that our darlings need supervision, that tag and chase are but scaled down versions of deadlier grownup pursuits. Weekends I hear the roar of college kids driven mad by boys chasing a leather ball up and down the grass, learning, my bosses tell me with straight faces, leadership skills. *2001* got it right, with its jawbone-turned-space station: we're dressed-up apes, and if "of such is the kingdom of God," Mother Nature help us all.

〰 MOSQUITOES

Where I grew up, mosquitoes are a year-round thing, and even Santa Claus wears bug spray when he visits South Carolina. So I was delighted to discover that mosquitoes are a sometime thing in the Valley of Virginia. Not that they don't live here. Down by the James River, where the land gets flat and boggy, they're nasty. But for large stretches of the valley, mosquitoes are as rare as cockroaches, thanks to terrain. Everything's so up and down in the valley water hasn't the chance to pause for long, and a mosquito can't breed in running water. People being people, we try to ruin a good thing, damming creeks, clogging gutters, filling birdbaths, and in general encouraging the making of mosquitoes. But it's a bad summer when, knock on wood, I'm bitten more than twice. Edward, raised here, thinks summer means bare legs, bare backs, and evenings outdoors. Little does he know, and long may he remain ignorant.

Walk Lexington's streets, and you'll notice there are few screened porches. You just don't need them. Out in the country, you'll find more, but they are to keep the flies away, those having plagued our farmers ever since they decided to raise cattle in a big way and leave the cow pats for the flies to wine and dine and procreate upon. On still summer afternoons the west side of my brick farmhouse would be speckled with thousands of flies, warming themselves and waiting for us to set the picnic table and invite them over for supper. Lexington's city fathers wisely banished cattle, so that the worst we have to fear evenings are the wasps, most of which are fairly well mannered even given a brush off, provided it be gentle.

Screens were perfected in the late nineteenth century, just when science was determining that mosquitoes, at least the female *Anopheles*, were no mere nuisance but rather a public-health hazard, being carriers of tiny *Plasmodium* parasites responsible for malaria. We Americans today for the most part remain blissfully unaware of malaria, thanks to its stateside eradication after World War II. But it has killed perhaps more people than any other disease. Even today, it kills one- to three-million people, many of them children in Africa. And well into the twentieth century, malaria was a major health threat in the United States. Much of the country was malarial, and, while no one knew for sure what caused it, malaria was associated with swamps and bogs, which led a disenchanted-with-America Charles Dickens in 1842 to describe "the detestable morass called Cairo, [Illinois,]" as "a breeding-place of fever, ague, and death. . . . A dismal swamp, on which the half-built houses rot away . . . and teeming, then, with rank unwholesome vegetation, in whose baleful shade the wretched wanderers who are tempted hither, droop, and die, and lay their bones; the hateful Mississippi circling and eddying before it, and turning off upon its southern course a slimy monster hideous to behold; a hotbed of disease, an ugly sepulchre, a grave uncheered by any gleam of promise: a place without one single quality, in earth or air or water, to commend it."

In Dickens's day, malaria's undoubted cause was bad air, *mala aria* in Italian, "caused by the effluvia rising from wet lands," as Virginia farmer and Rebel firebrand Edmund Ruffin explained to antebellum Americans in his condemnation of "a mania for building mill-ponds . . . producing noxious exhalations, and autumnal diseases." Night airs were regarded as especially dangerous, and our ancestors kept their windows closed to avoid breathing the night's foul vapors, which led Founding Fathers John Adams and Benjamin Franklin to quarrel over an open window when forced to share a bed in New Brunswick, New Jersey, in 1776. Adams reports that, "The Window was open, and I, who was an invalid and afraid of the Air in the night [blowing upon me], shut it close. Oh! says Franklin don't shut the Window. We shall be suffocated. I answered I was afraid of the Evening Air. Dr. Franklin replied, the Air within this Chamber will soon be, and indeed now worse than that without Doors: come! open the Window and come to bed, and I will convince you: I believe you are not acquainted with my Theory of Colds." Adams falls asleep while Franklin discourses, and only half remembers his friend's theory that the stale air of rooms, filled with the effluvia of humans, is more dangerous than night air. But Adams isn't converted; he writes of Franklin that "he fell a Sacrifice at last, not to the Stone but to his own Theory; having caught the violent Cold, which finally choaked him, by sitting for some hours at a Window, with the cool Air blowing upon him."

Which may be why we "catch" colds to this day, as we've been doing at least since Shakespeare, one of whose characters remarks in the *Comedy of Errors* that, "Let him walk from whence he came, lest he catch cold on's [on his] feet," while King Lear's Fool laments, "Nay, an thou canst not smile as the wind sits, thou'lt catch cold shortly." Despite Shakespeare, the skeptical Franklin thought, "*no one ever* catches the disorder we call a cold from cold air." Colds, he thought, came from lack of sweating, since sweating was the body's way of getting rid of putrefying matter caused by our internal heat. Trapped in a room with other people, our bodies steep in a stew of putrid air, so that, "Scarce any air abroad so unwholesome as air in a close room often breathed." Not until the end of the nineteenth century was the miasmal theory of fevers replaced by Pasteur's germ theory. And not until then were window screens readily available to keep out the mosquitoes, which replaced night air as the cause of malaria. But by 1900 more and more Americans were listening to Matthew Arnold's invitation, "Come to the window, sweet is the night-air!" And who of us wouldn't thank Chicagoan John Golding, awarded in 1884 a patent for his metallic screening to be used in doors and windows, before whom we slept summers under mosquito netting in rooms with the windows closed?

Golding may have ended my great-grandparents' stifling summer nights in Carolina, but here in Virginia we have no need of screens, and summer means dragging a mattress out onto porch or grass and sleeping under the stars, your arm under the head of your child as the two of you trace the satellite that sails slower and steadier than a firefly across the sky each night at 9:15, he drifting off as the Summer Triangle rides high overhead, and you lying awake, listening to his breathing and feeling the night grow cool, and your thoughts tangled sad and happy at the same time until you too close your eyes, the Milky Way your night light. Unless, of course, the rare whining mosquito drowns out your child's gentle breathing. Then it's the debate you never win: swat at the damn thing or let it bite and have done with it.

Quinine, of course, was malaria's miracle cure. Revealed to Europeans by the Incas of South America, the bark of the chinchona tree, Perúvian or Jesuit bark, was the only real cure the world had. But that fact didn't stop people from assuming there were others, especially since quinine can cause "headache, deafness, noises in the ears, . . . nausea, delirium, or coma," according to an 1866 medical book, which nevertheless went on to prescribe it for malaria, yellow fever, cholera, measles, scarlet fever, whooping cough, gangrene, scurvy, tetanus, epilepsy, and insanity. And the stuff tasted horrible, which is why someone invented the gin and tonic, two or three of which I take as a precaution before venturing outside summer evenings.

Edward won't drink them. He thinks they taste terrible, and his school's convinced him alcohol's such an evil that I've given up buying it when he's with me, preferring to sneak it into the house like an alcoholic pretending he's on the wagon. Fortunately Edward likes sassafras tea with lots of sugar and milk. And sassafras is so effective in curing malaria that Englishman John Gerard called it the ague tree in his 1597 *Herbal.* Evenings Edward sips his tea and I my tonic, and together we defeat malaria and melancholy.

Equally effective daylight prophylactics against both malaria and melancholy are sunflowers. Matthew Fontaine Maury, after whom my local river is named, may have achieved worldwide fame for charting the seas' currents. Far happier, however, was his notion that planting sunflowers in Washington, D.C., could provide a vegetable barrier to malarial fevers rising from the Potomac River. He even persuaded the Italians to sow huge plantations of sunflowers, whose descendants still make beautiful the fields of Europe. And thanks to Maury, every summer, Edward and I plant a screen of giant sunflowers at the end of the garden; neither of us has yet contracted malaria.

Maury was vague as to the exact nature of the sunflower's remarkable powers. But not so George Perkins Marsh, who, demonstrating the curative power of trees, explains, "that the great swamps of Virginia and the Carolinas, in climates nearly similar to that of Italy, are healthy even to the white man, so long as the forests in and around them remain, but become very insalubrious when the woods are felled." Virginia's Dismal Swamp was a misnomer, Marsh celebrating "the sweetness and wholesome character of the water, and the entire freedom of its few inhabitants from malarious diseases. This purity is ascribed to the influence of the juniper tree," the trees having "robbed the atmosphere of the enormous quantity of carbonic acid it contained, and thereby transformed it into respirable air." Fortunately for Marsh, he lived before the malarial mosquito replaced miasma, because the Dismal Swamp, into which I ventured one August for reasons I'm still not sufficiently clear on, is as thick as South Carolina with mosquitoes, which goes some ways toward explaining Marsh's cogent observation regarding "its few inhabitants."

President Ronald Reagan's killer-tree hypothesis was, it seems, erroneous, which is just as well, since the juniper, or cedar tree, is ubiquitous in the valley. But such trees do more than merely cleanse the air. Confederate doctor Francis Porcher explains in expert scientific-ese that pine forests filled with "miles of surface bristling with good conductors" must affect the ambient electricity. "The terebinthinate odor of the tree, some electrical influence of its long, spearlike leaves, a certain modification of 'ozone' ... are severally esteemed to modify the atmosphere and diminish the effects of malaria. They also create a mechanical barrier to the ingress of malaria, and hence the pine land residences, though contemned for their sterile aspect, have proved a blessing to the Southern planters in affording a comparatively safe refuge from the unhealthy emanations of the neighboring plantations." Behind our barn grew just such a mechanical barrier, a grove of white pines, in whose terebinthinate odors I used to delight while chewing on a long, spearlike leaf, reminding me as they did of the pine barrens of my youth.

The mosquito's motto may well be, *Et in arcadia ego*, and while Edward and I walked the paths I'd cut through the pines, I would ponder the dilemma that Marsh raised regarding trees. "The foliage of trees and of other vegetables exercises a chemical as well as a mechanical effect upon the atmosphere, and some, who allow that forests may intercept the circulation of the miasmatic effluvia of swampy soils, or even render them harmless by decomposing them, contend, nevertheless, that they are themselves active causes of the production of malaria." Such differences of opinion led to the rise and fall of the ailanthus tree as a malarial barrier. Ailanthus mania seized America in the 1830s, when thousands of the oriental-looking trees were planted for shade in cities, their rapid growth supposedly absorbing malarial miasmas. When people noticed that the male trees' leaves smelled bad, they decided the tree caused rather than prevented malaria and down they came, landscape gardener Andrew Jackson Downing leading the attack against "an usurper in rather bad *odor* at home, which has come over to this land of liberty, under the garb of utility, to make foul the air, with its pestilent breath, and devour the soil, with its intermeddling roots—a tree that has the fair outside and the treacherous heart of the Asiatics. . . . Down with the ailanthus! therefore, we cry with the populace."

One hundred and eighty years later, descendants of those ailanthus had seeded themselves on the ragged border of my pine forest, and Edward and I declared war on them, me chainsawing the larger ones, which raised their branches in arthritic horror at my approach, while Edward slew with a stick dozens of fragile newsprung trees, whose branchless trunks rose from the grass like lightning rods. Satisfied, a hundred felled trees at our feet, we paused, and then I heard, low and insidious, the whine of a female mosquito intent on blood.

SPRING EPHEMERALS

Dispirited by months of glum, gray, gloomy Virginia winter, I seek signs of light and life in bogs harboring skunk cabbage (*Symplocarpus foetidus*), which I first learned of as a child reading about exotic northern forests where these plants grew, generating their own inner heat to melt through the snow. They linger here and there in the county, leftovers from the Ice Age, blooming as early as January, though I often miss them, forgetting until they sprout their cabbagelike, oversized leaves in marshy fields. Their green mounds scattered amid the brown wreckage of last year's cattails raise hopes of winter's end, which the spring peepers (*Pseudacris crucifer*) that share the wet field with the cabbages officially announce in March. I've seldom seen these small frogs marked with a black cross upon their back, but every spring the males surprise me, gathering in wet spots to outpeep their rivals and so gain the right to piggyback their girlfriends, which is how my father explained the froggy rituals we observed as children. Almost as well concealed as peepers are skunk-cabbage flowers hidden in the leaf litter of streams and bogs, their dark, chubby spadices dotted with tiny white flowers winking at you from within a swollen hood of green and purple leaves that speaks of sex and other mysteries. So to does the skunk cabbage's funky, skunky odor, said to attract the flies that pollinate it and the reason Linnaeus named it *foetidus*, meaning smelly, as in our word *fetid*.

In March, the dandelion-like coltsfoot (*Tussilago farfara*) pushes up through the crushed gravel of road shoulders, before even its heart-shaped leaves appear, the first public proof that spring is coming. An invasive weed from Europe, coltsfoot was presumably brought by settlers who used to smoke or chew it to cure asthma and coughs. Nearly as early is the native bloodroot (*Sanguinaria canadensis*), whose white, six-or-more-petaled flowers rise up out of its still-rolled-up leaves as if from a sheltering cloak. Named for the orange-red sap that freely flows from its rootlike rhizome, bloodroot has been used to treat various skin disorders, despite government disapproval and sometime prosecution. The evanescent flowers die a day or two after pollination, dropping their petals one by one as their leaves unfold, the ground around them littered with discarded beauty.

Of flowering trees, shadbush (*Amelanchier*) is perhaps the earliest, Edward and I competing to see who's first to spot the small tree's white drift of flowers against the still gray forest backdrop. This burst of color gladdens my winter-weary heart, not least of all because it heralds the running of the shad, whose spring spawning brings them upriver. Three to eight pounds and bony as hell, shad are held by many to be better tasting than salmon, and shad roe is to die for, according to yet others; every spring my father and I would make a pilgrimage to a now sadly defunct restaurant in Frogmore, South Carolina, for roe and grits. The Blue Ridge stopped Virginia's shad from getting any farther upriver than Lynchburg, but sometimes, when the shadbush blooms, a local store will have a bedraggled shad or beat-up-looking clump of roe, and I will buy it, hoping against hope that, this time, it will take me back down memory's river, to when I sat beside my father, who, smacking his lips, remarked, "I wonder what the poor people are eating tonight." Come summer, the shadbush changes names, becoming the service or Juneberry and its sometimes blah, sometimes blueberry-tasting red berries ripening.

A bit after the shadbush, the still leafless redbud (*Cercis canadensis*) blooms pink, its trunk and branches lined with bunches of tiny flowers. My father called this the Judas tree, claiming it was the tree Judas Iscariot hanged himself on after betraying Jesus, the flowers reddening from shame or Judas's blood. How an American tree wound up in Roman Judea I never thought to ask. English colonists brought the legend with them; in England a cousin of our redbud, *Cercis siliquastrum*, native to southern Europe and the Levant, was called the Judas tree. However, the French call it *arbre de Judée*, or the tree of Judea, suggesting that "Judas tree" is a mistranslation. To confuse matters, the Spanish call it *árbol del amor*, probably after its heart-shaped leaves and red flowers. For me, though, redbud is a salad tree, its easily harvested flowers both edible and beautiful. I mix handfuls of the bright pink buds with watercress (*Nasturtium officinale*), whose rosettes of bright green leaves have grown large enough to be picked by the time the redbuds bloom. Celia has a bounty of watercress growing in the creek behind her cabin; they are plants that require no care at all and that offer their leaves every time I walk that way in summer, their peppery bite a reminder that they belong to the mustard family, which, like watercress, hails from the Old World. Field mustard's (*Brassica rapa*) yellow blossoms add a splash of color to a salad, as do the purple, white, gray, and yellow flowers of violets (*Viola* species) I gather in moist woods.

Blooming the same time as the redbud is the flowering dogwood (*Cornus florida*), whose small, yellowish flowers also appear before the leaves. These are surrounded by what we mistakenly think of as flower petals, four white—or, rarely in the wild, pink—leaves, or bracts. Why it's a dogwood nobody really knows, some saying it disparages the useless berries, *dog* once denoting such inedible food. Others think it a corruption of dagwood, dag being a pointed object, as in dagger. Yet others think it refers to bathing dogs in water in which dogwood had been soaked. But nearly everyone knows Jesus was crucified upon a dogwood cross. Ashamed, the tree shrank too small to make another cross, its four petals in shame formed both the cross's shape and Christ's wounds, and the embarrassed fruit recalled the crown of thorns. This description applies to the American dogwood; the European dogwood, or cornelian cherry (*Cornus mas*) to which the Romans would have had access, has small yellow flowers that look nothing like their American cousin's.

But the real flower show is lower down, among last year's leaves, in what in a month will be shade too deep for flowers but which is, for a brief moment, perfect, sunny soil. On Sugar Creek's fifty-foot hillsides, flowers there are by the thousands, carpets of foot-high trillium (*Trillium grandiflorum*), a white and green cascade spilling downhill into the creek. Closer to town on Brushy Hill, the carpet is more worn, a threadbare quiltwork of white trillium and the shorter but striking maroon wake robin (*T. sessile*), so loud a color that it woke the robins, the settlers said. Jacks-in-the-pulpit (*Arisaema triphyllum*) preach the gospel of spring to nodding ferns accompanied by fern fiddles. The easiest show to catch is on the east-facing slopes in the woods behind the colleges, with fewer trillium and jacks, perhaps because it's drier, but rich with its own weave of Dutchman's britches (*Dicentra cucullaria*) drying in the breeze, yellow trout lilies (*Erythronium americanum*) with leaves as speckled as a fish, spring beauty (*Claytonia*) and its pink-streaked delights, wild geranium (*Geranium maculatum*) with its fine-lined, pale purple flowers, chickweed (*Stellaria pubera*) and its solar system's worth of knobby stamens crowning each ten-petalled star, mayapple (*Podophyllum peltatum*) with its twin umbrellas, bellwort (*Uvularia*) and its nodding yellow flowers half wrapped in green, tart-leaved wood sorrel (*Oxalis*), and wild ginger (*Asarum canadense*) with its shy flowers hid beneath heart-shaped leaves. Elsewhere, along North Mountain, I've stumbled upon Virginia's gaudiest flowers, the pink lady's slipper (*Cypripedium acaule*), and in the Blue Ridge, hillsides of yellow lady's slipper (*Cypripedium parviflorum*), their vein-fretted pouches swollen like cows' udders, luring my prurient gaze and bees bent on nectar. Vulgar orchids worthy of Georgia O'Keeffe, they grow more scarce yearly as greedy gardeners carry them away to the valley's too sweet soil where the fungi they depend on cannot thrive. These are the flowers to come upon with someone you're seducing, their sweet swell cousin to that filling your companion's jeans, the fissure between Mecca for the devout. Oh to be a bee, trapped for delicious hours within those swelling, swollen membranes.

Enough. Flowers were once God's gift to us, a jeu d'esprit of love. But come the Enlightenment, in E. E. Cummings's words, "the doting fingers of prurient philosophers pinched and poked" the earth, "the naughty thumb of science prodded [its] beauty," and we discovered that, yes, indeed, flowers, which heretofore had been but beautiful, were sexual organs splayed out for all to see. Erasmus Darwin salaciously described the loves of multiwived and multihusbanded plants, his polyandrous, polygamous poetry inspiring Coleridge and Wordsworth to take themselves to the woods and Darwin's grandson Charles to discover natural selection.

I found myself, one Easter weekend long ago, in a garden next to a church, admiring the bee-stung pink and purple azaleas, echoed in the crepe de chine blossoming round my girlfriend's legs, thinking less of Christ's resurrection than my own. Now that I'm old, the girlfriend gone, the azaleas in another state, I wonder what spring flowers bring, gaudy, momentary exuberances that they are. Most are doomed to rot, unfulfilled and sterile, like we who go headlong into the abyss, frustrated, wishing what might have been had been, and hoping better for our children. Should our children chance upon a spring ephemeral when we are gone, may they think on us, food for flowers, and, sniffing deep the loam and rot, the bloom and the decay, remember us, remember us.

⑴⑴ FLYING FRASS

Slow summer days could once find me in the scruffy woods below the house, shaded by white pines (*Pinus strobus*) planted some twenty years ago, counting the yearly whorls of branches. Among them black locusts (*Robinia pseudoacacia*) had quickly grown up, many dead, killed by insects and fungi, the latter sprouting woody shelves along the trunks. New plants continued to spring up, however, from the tangled network of locust roots running throughout the woods, and it was these I eyed, sitting, back against a pine. The locusts' young, tender branches were crowded with aphids busily sucking the nutrient-rich phloem the locust leaves were shipping back to the roots. It takes a lot of watery plant sap to make an aphid lunch, and the small bugs excrete large quantities of sugar water through two tailpipes on their hind ends. You can watch them close up with a magnifying glass, pear-shaped creatures a tenth of an inch long crouched head down on thin black legs and, every now and then, raising and lowering their rears in unison and expelling plant juice. As there are dozens of kinds of aphids and they congregate on all sorts of plants, your chances of finding them in your garden are good, as any gardener who has cursed them knows. Before killing, however, watch them. The prodigious numbers cloaking the branches in red, brown, black, green, gray, or yellow blankets are often all Virgin Marys, females producing children without sex. Without male chromosomes, the offspring are all female, and so it goes, generation after generation of happy miracle. Should you find an aphid colony, your chances of witnessing a virgin birth are good, and I have seen many baby aphids born by mothers too busy grazing to take note. These women are all wingless, though, stuck on the plant they're born on, incapable of waddling far.

Cowlike, wingless aphids are food-on-the-hoof for plenty of bugs, including the ladybugs, green lacewings, and predatory gall midges sold to aphid-weary gardeners. What these hapless women need is an army of Amazons, which is just what Mother Nature provided them, in the guise of ants, who guard their aphid herds as well as milk them. The ants run up and down the branches like nervous cowgirls, patrolling for rustlers, every so often stopping to stroke an aphid's butt until she produces a drink. It's hard to see this close up, since you're likely to scare the ants if you get too close, and you have to get close to make sense of what you're seeing, but you can do it. What's easier, once you've actually seen virgin birth and an aphid milkshake close up, is to use binoculars to watch godlike the bigger branch.

Aphids produce such quantities of this sweet and sticky liquid that, when they expel it, they do so with enough force to throw it away from them, to escape being mired in their own excrement. If you give enough excreting aphids enough time, they will produce a rain of excrement that covers whatever lies beneath their tree, as car owners have found to their chagrin. Such weeping trees were once famous, since no one knew before a hundred years ago why they wept or where their tears came from. The miraculously appearing sweet was called honeydew, and the Roman Pliny couldn't decide "Whether it is that this liquid is the sweat of the heavens, or whether a saliva emanating from the stars, or a juice exuding from the air while purifying itself." He thought it the source of bee honey (which is primarily plant nectar), and there is in fact a dark, oddly flavored honey produced by bees collecting honeydew from aphids and scale insects that is today produced primarily in Germany's Black Forest. Later Europeans, however, thought considerably less of honeydew than did Pliny, and Victorian Englishman John Murray thought it caused by "'Some blight, imported on the wings of the wind, by which the ambient air is parched, while a crippled and diseased vegetation transpires from its leafage the saccharine exudation,'" adding that, "as the eagles will collect where the carcase is, so aphides congregate where the leaves are imbued with this morbid nectar." Honeydew, then, was not the product of aphids; it merely attracted them. And too much honeydew could cause mildew, which comes to us from Old English *meledeaw,* or honeydew.

Unappetizing though it may be to imagine eating aphid poop, you should try it next time you find a tree coated in honeydew: just run your finger over a leaf and you'll feel it picking up the sticky coating. Pop it in your mouth and lick—you're eating star spit, the sweat of gods. Nor are you the only thing willing to eat honeydew. The ants on my locust branch are too. Ant farming of aphid herds is widespread, some ants even sheltering aphid eggs overwinter underground and moving them to their proper plant source come spring. Thanks to fossil amber from the Baltic, scientists know that ants and aphids were associating with each other as long as fifty million years ago. Many think the symbiotic relationship developed from an initially predatory one, as ants gradually replaced eating aphids with milking them. The ants can, and sometimes do, eat their charges, but that makes them no different from the local dairy farmers, who sell their older cows for meat.

Most insect poop is more solid than aphid honeydew. It's called frass, and sometimes so many caterpillars are at work in the trees that you can hear it falling like a gentle rain upon the ground. Scientists use such frass falls to estimate the number of insects, which can be legion when, say, the gypsy moths are gnawing their way through a forest. Caterpillar frass is relatively firm and easy to handle and, looked at closely, quite lovely. While experts can identify what species shat what frass, we lesser mortals merely muse at how excrement, shaped and sculpted by its passage through an insect's gut, can resemble a work of art.

While most caterpillars are content to let their loads drop where they will, one heaves its frass into the air. The two-inch-long yellow and green caterpillar of the fairly common silver-spotted skipper (*Epargyreus clarus*) builds tents out of the leaves of the trees it feeds on, black locusts like the one I used to sit under being his favorite. Crawling out of its tent at night, it feeds voraciously. And when it needs to relieve itself, it shoots its frass up, up, and away into the air, so that predatory wasps, which home in on the smell of frass, can't find the caterpillar. They call it scatapulting.

MY CIVIL WAR

Lexington is the Valhalla of the Confederacy, with both Thomas "Stonewall" Jackson and Robert E. Lee buried here, and, nursery of more than eight hundred Confederate officers, the Virginia Military Institute one of the town's two colleges. Twenty years of residence have accustomed me to much about Virginia, but I can still recall my shock at walking into the chapel at Washington and Lee University and finding, where one would expect an altar to Christ, the recumbent body of Robert E. Lee, asleep like Arthur, waiting for his country's call. Downstairs, a dynasty of Roberts fills the crypt, each succeeding son's neck hung with an ever bigger, ever heavier Roman numeral. Next door, in VMI's churchlike Jackson Memorial Hall, where saints might climb to heaven in the religious paintings I grew up with, the Corps of Cadets charges toward a glory more martial than angelic in a painted recreation of the Battle of New Market. Outside, having climbed down from the state flag, a larger-than-life Virginia mourns her dead from the same battle, ten young men remembered every May 15 when their mystical descendants in the cadet corps march before her. And while the church I grew up in was named after St. Michael, the original Christian soldier, Lexingtonians worship in the Robert E. Lee Memorial Episcopal Church.

In front of VMI's barracks, Stonewall Jackson, his jacket blown back by an imaginary wind, stares south toward Lexington's Stonewall Jackson Memorial Cemetery, where his body is buried beneath another statue, by the same artist who sculpted the sleeping Lee. Watched over by Jackson are markers to his second wife, Mary Anna Morrison, their daughters, and descendants, two military sons among them, one dead in France in World War II, all the proof one needs, if proof be needed, that the winds of war that ruffled Jackson's jacket still blow. Confederate loyalists scale the iron fence guarding Jackson's family to plant the Stars and Bars, and others toss over lemons, which legend claims Jackson loved, and pursed-mouth historians discount. A smaller marble stone marks Jackson's original burial site, within a low iron paling, near where his first wife, Elinor Junkin Jackson, dead in childbirth, still lies, her husband taken from her by adoring southerners.

Women mourning at Jackson's original grave, Lexington, Virginia, cemetery, ca. 1862.
Courtesy of Virginia Military Institute Archives

Her sister Margaret Junkin married VMI founder and Stonewall Jackson's future chief of staff J. T. L. Preston, but, according to some biographers, might more readily have married Jackson, so close were he and she, had the Presbyterian Church not forbade marriage between a widower and his dead wife's sister. During their raid on Lexington, Yankee soldiers told her of their visiting Jackson's grave, which prompted her to write "Stonewall Jackson's Grave," in which she describes "A simple, sodded mound of earth, / Without a line above it; / With only daily votive flowers / To prove that any love it" visited by "countless pilgrim-feet" of "weeping women" and "Contending armies." Long gone to fame and adulation is the simple, sodded mound of earth that weeping women, including Margaret Preston, visited, and the grave she knew lies empty. She herself lies in her husband's family plot, so chockablock with graves that bodies must be stacked underground like Lincoln logs. She lies under a stone her sons erected defining her as wife and daughter, shaded by an enormous white oak, just able, on the nights that ghosts rise, to catch Jackson's long, lean form, sculpted by a man named Valentine, standing beyond a wall of gravestones.

But what, when all is said and done, is one dead general among the six hundred thousand men who died with him in the war? Jackson commands an army of the dead, including 144 Confederate veterans who lie with him in Lexington's most famous cemetery. Fellow Confederate Levi Miller lies, unvisited, in Evergreen Cemetery, the black graveyard a mile away, as Jim Crow flies, from where his white comrades in arm lie honored by heavy metal Confederate Crosses of Honor. Born a slave, Miller accompanied his owner to war, where he so distinguished himself as a soldier he won a pension from Virginia after the war. Edward and I first discovered Miller when the kite we were flying in the neighboring middle-school playground wrapped itself around one of the cemetery's cedars and collapsed. We found it hiding behind a large stone marker with CSA chiseled in it, and relearned that history, concerning people as it does, is decidedly odd.

Not that Miller was the most prominent of Lexington's black Confederates. That curious distinction goes to James Lewis, one of Stonewall Jackson's several wartime servants. Whether free or a slave, and no one's sure, Lewis has entered Lost Cause lore as the embodiment of the faithful retainer. When he died, Lewis was buried in an unmarked grave in Lexington's "Colored Cemetery," and white

Jackson's second resting place, Stonewall Jackson Memorial Cemetery, Lexington, Virginia. Courtesy of Virginia Military Institute Archives

city fathers are said to have rejected an English offer to raise Lewis a gravestone the year they celebrated erecting Valentine's statue to Jackson. They are also said to have sold the cemetery off to developers without ensuring the dead were reinterred in the new Evergreen Cemetery. Who knows if the televisions and telephones of those who live above them disturb the sleeping Lewis and his neighbors so that they walk Lexington's benighted streets, seeking a decency denied in life and death?

Be not deceived; I am a somewhat loyal son of the South. My mother wore every Sunday to church a brooch with two crossed locks of hair, the boys who'd grown them remembered in our church's monument: "How grand a fame this marble watches o'er! / Their Wars behind them— God's great Peace before." Grown, I pilgrimed to the banks of Bull Run, a not-worth-the-mentioning Virginia stream, had not Jackson earned his nickname Stonewall there in the first battle at the site where one of the boys whose locks my mother treasured died. The other died in a still extant dirt ditch under Jackson's command in the second battle of Bull Run.

But I was corrupted young. As a Cub Scout, learning a marvelously martial song I had been instructed to keep secret, I marched up and down my sandbox, imagining the watch fires of a hundred circling camps, only to have my mother yank me off stage in the middle of my singing to the local PTA Harriet Beecher Stowe's "Battle Hymn of the Republic," whose lyrics have had for me, ever since, a deliciously subversive flavor. And now that I live north enough to grow lilacs, I remember each April 15 what a transplanted New York high-school teacher taught me forty years ago in South Carolina about the "lilac-bush tall-growing, with heart-shaped leaves of rich green, / With many a pointed blossom, rising, delicate, with the perfume strong I love," though my students seem taken aback when I arrive in class "With delicate-color'd blossoms, and heart-shaped leaves of rich green" and read Walt Whitman's too-long poem to Lincoln when income tax is due. Interminable the debates my students have among states rights, slavery, and preserving the Union as causes for the war, and all too few think, whatever the war's causes, that defense of slavery puts us forever in the wrong.

Moral superiority would be easier without Levi Miller. Or Jim Lewis. Or the frustrated passion of Margaret Junkin and Thomas Jackson. Hopeless English teacher that I am, I remember Shakespeare, who preferred the personal over the ideological as cause for England's Wars of the Roses; Yeats, who thought Paris's love for Helen reason enough to celebrate Troy's fall; George W. Bush's "He tried to kill my dad" as justification for war with Saddam Hussein; and I wonder if I'm fit to teach our youth.

ᯤ MIGRATION

In fall, when cold fronts blow south from Canada, blueing the skies and leaving the air fresh and clear with a crisp hint of cold to come, the monarchs appear, jibbing, tacking, and running before the wind like miniature galleons. Then I walk McElwee Road, following the creek up its gentle, as yet unmcmansioned valley, with cattle still grazing on either side. Trending southwest with the Shenandoah, the butterflies coast by in orange waves, spreading east and west up over the hills' crests into Back Draft and the Turnpike's valleys and fanning out farther east and west in a great thin blanket stitched by a million nearly mindless living threads. They obey a call that stirs the birds and trees, and even humans, though so attenuated in us that we feel but a vague discontent and irritation that lasts until mid March.

Looking left and right, I count one, two, three, four, then five; then three more, eight; two over there, ten; and three, no four—no that's a bird—but three, makes eleven; and on and on and on, until I tire of being cerebral and run with the wind and the waves of butterflies and flap my arms and would fly south with them. We would fly down past Lexington and Buchanan and Roanoke and swoop up the thousand-foot escarpment into the New River's broad pastures, heading south and west with the mountains, following valley and stream ever higher into the great, grand tangle of the Smokies and pour in torrents through the wind gaps and join the orange rivers overlaid upon the Tennessee and Mississippi valleys. All of us head south and west in greater and greater numbers through Mississippi and Louisiana and into Texas where we overwhelm the border guards and crash across the Rio Grande in a river grander than anything carved by water and further south and west into the ten-thousand-foot-high mountains west of Mexico City where we rope the fir trees in a treasure undreamt of by Humphrey Bogart mucking for gold beneath us.

We've all read the stories of the 1975 discovery by Ken Brugger of this treasure of the Sierra Madre, a treasure long known, of course, to the locals who, in 1975, learned at last where their monarchs disappeared to every spring. Tracking the telltale DNA of the milkweeds monarchs feed on, entomologist Lincoln Brower, who teaches just over the Blue Ridge at Sweet Briar College, discovered that the monarchs flying north from the Sierras into the United States mate and die on the Gulf Coast, their offspring flying north to the Great Lakes, mating and dying there, and their children flying east into the Atlantic seaboard, including the Shenandoah Valley. And it is the children of these monarchs, four generations removed from Mexico, that tug me southward with them in the fall.

I can hide indoors and ignore the colored flags flying through Lexington toward the south and warmth. But lose myself though I will in the mindless day-to-day of work, when I awake on a morning and hear overhead the mournful call of Canada geese Veeing south, I float away to winter mornings fifty years ago when my brother and sisters and I waited unhappily at the end of our driveway in the cold dark morning for the yellow school bus while overhead, above the lowering clouds, the geese called to our souls to come with them. Long dead, those ever so great-great-grand progenitors of today's callers still sing within my head, heralds of hopes lost, abandoned, and forsaken on the long road that brought me to a kitchen window out of which I look and dream of what might have been. The geese have taken to living here year round, feeding by day on dairy farmers' cornfields, and flocking at night to the safety of the Maury River and countless farm and drainage ponds scattered like sapphires through the valley. I pass by such a pond on my morning runs with my dog, and, if my timing's right, she and I see the large birds flying up and over the dam like bomber squadrons, large and dark against the winter's dull dawn, calling one to the other as they wing toward the brightening east. But I am earthbound by more than winglessness, and Scooby is tethered to me, bark though she might at the heralds, as through their scattered droppings we make our way back to my chosen reality.

My backyard bird feeder reminds me each fall that the anchors holding me here can be pulled up or cut, my yard a way station for those who pass from here to there, blue jays and redbirds and chickadees and finches and titmice and bird fanciers only know what all congregating in noisy jubilee outside the dining room window. We watch from inside our comfortable prison, the dog and cat stalking them, Scooby hurling herself at the window through which I fear she'll crash one day and Socks patiently watching from behind the philodendron's leaves. My senses dulled, only the most extravagant of migrators catch my attention. But even I could not miss the evening spectacle that Edward discovered in downtown Lexington when we went to post a letter and he saw a giant flock of chimney swifts swirl, darken, and coalesce into an aerial maelstrom that sank round and round and down into an abandoned chimney. For several nights we watched them; then they were gone, winging south toward the Amazon.

Virginia herself has migrated, drifting north over the millennia so that I stand nearly thirty-eight degrees north of the equator, more than seven thousand miles north of where, somewhere in the latitude of Brazil, geologists say the rocks beneath me were laid down 450 million years ago. These, the scientists say, are remnants of tropical tidal flats, mostly muddy limestone to the eye, but here and there in Rockbridge County, thick with trilobites, clamlike brachiopods, snail-like ammonites, starfish-on-a-stalk crinoids, all long ago tossed in heaps by vanished waves, buried and turned to stone, and slowly exposed by ever colder rains and snows as the North American continental plate slowly drifted from warm to cold.

Not that it hasn't been colder here before this. The Virginia winters that depress me and drive birds and bugs across the sea are balmy compared to those that blew south off the ice sheets creeping south from Hudson Bay to Pennsylvania. Then all that creatures could fled south and east to whatever warmth they could find, even the plants hopscotching at vegetable speeds toward the sun. Those who know such things say that there were Arctic barrens, tundra, treelines, and frozen wastes here. Tucked into corners of the valley are descendants of these migrants, cranberries that properly should be in Massachusetts, moosewood and paper birch blown here from New York, sphagnum bogs from Maine, skunk cabbage from New Hampshire. Farther south and west, where the mountains rise higher, balsam firs and red spruce with nowhere else to go grasp to ever more precarious mountain perches as global warming threatens to drive them to extinction.

But winter is no time for sympathizing with these Arctic waifs. My north-facing front yard, in shadow nearly all day long throughout winter, stays as ice- and snowbound as Montreal for weeks after the rest of Massie Street is clear. Here Edward and I build snowmen to last a month, keeping a sharp eye out for wandering polar bears and snowblind Eskimos, and here is where the perfect-variety-for-this-region plants regularly die. Inside my house, tropical memories etiolate, wan and pale, leggy and long, longing for sun, the Canadian hemlocks outside their south-facing windows enough to frighten their chlorophyll into hiding.

Fall darkens and dampens into what the my students call the gray days, when the clouds hang lower than the mountains and the sun is dreary and dissipated. Sound carries farther in moist air, and in the dark hours before dawn I lie in bed and listen to the hum of traffic from the interstate three miles away. Lee Hi Truck stop is always open, and I sometimes go there when I simply cannot sleep. Dead though the town be, the truck stop goes all night, and tired though I be, Lee Hi can waken even me. Outside its rows of trucks are lit up with motors purring, inside its booths filled with cowboy-booted, big-bellied truckers on their ways to somewhere else, smoking and drinking coffee and bullshitting about routes and weather and food in what must be, I know in my saner moments, a wearying and soul-numbing job, but which in the soul's three o'clock in the morning promises an open road and the freedom to be whatever I resolve to be. Oh, to be rolling south with the warmth into Florida's great, tropic-reaching peninsula, a thousand miles and more down to the Keys, where America ends and it never freezes. The gray-haired mom and pop snowbirds slowly poking south toward Floridian condos I mocked in my youthful days seem sager now, and I wonder what living in a Winnebago is like.

Truckers, retirees, birds, bugs, and monarchs trouble the stagnant waters of my soul, and spying a patch of orange disappearing round the bend or over the hill, or hearing a goose crying southwards in the dark or the distant hum of rubber against asphalt, I rouse myself and pace my cage and yearn for a time that never was and a soul and spirit strong enough to leap the moats and bend the bars of my self-imposed conformity and spread my wings and fly away, fly away.

RUNNING THE RIVER

Edward and I are lazying down the Maury River in a canoe I bought from the Livery after it started leaking too much to rent it out anymore. When the Maury swirling around our tennis-shoe clad feet reaches shoelace depth, it's time to start bailing, but, until then, we let the river hitch a ride with us. Between the mooing cows and murmuring river, afternoon sun and the beer in my gut, I'm half asleep and Edward's in charge, paddling this way and that across the river as he learns the hard way how to steer a canoe when your partner's too lazy to help. The murmuring in my ears becomes a little louder, more and more insistent, and my co-pilot is yelling, "Rapids, Daddy, rapids." Twenty years ago when I first came to Rockbridge County, I'd have been terrified; two beers earlier, I might have been attentive; but now I'm relaxed and happy that the river's decided to wake itself up a bit. I sit up, grab my paddle, and look downriver to where the Maury shallows out in a rock-bestrewn rapids perhaps fifty feet long and nowhere deeper than a cobble. We're going to scrape, but that's why the canoe leaks in the first place: it rubbed the Maury the wrong way once upon a time, and the river punched a hole in her just to let her know who's boss out here.

It was Matthew Fontaine Maury, charter of the oceans' currents, Confederate soldier and VMI professor, after whom Virginians renamed what until then had been the North River. Rising west of North Mountain where the Calfpasture and Little Calfpasture rivers combine, the Maury flows first through the four miles of rock-strewn Goshen Pass, which my black and blue butt remembers inner tubing one summer and which kayakers more successfully run when the water's up in winter. Once through the mountain, the Maury settles down, and wiggles forty contented miles through the Shenandoah Valley, cutting oxbows in the valley limestone to the puzzlement of geologists unused to such placid-river hallmarks in a mountain stream.

The current flows, first on this side of the river's bed, then on that, crossings-over marked by rapids or riffles. Nor does the current linger long on either side, driven by will or fate, inertia, gravity, or accident to switch sides every half mile or so. Where the current runs against the shore, the bank can be high, a thousand or more clambering, climb-me feet of rock. Edward and I explore those cliffs from time to time, sneaking across some absent farmer's field to gaze down upon the Maury, Edward heaving a cobble he's picked up from a fossil streambed laid down who knows how many years ago when the Maury ran a thousand feet of rock higher than it is today and all that rock from North Mountain to the Blue Ridge washed downriver to Virginia Beach, where I have sifted through my fingers sand that came from Lexington so long ago it had forgot its birth bed.

On the other side of the river, away from the current, the Maury builds point bars, sand and rock junkbeds, where everything that can get snagged—trees, fences, tires, tin roofs, canoes, dead cows, plastic bags—gets snagged. Here too, though, the river builds sand bluffs, just high enough above the water to look down and play king of the fish. Grassy picnic grounds when grazed by cattle, they're sunny enough for me to lie down on while Edward plays in the water, chasing fish and overturning rocks to see what lives beneath them.

And much still does, despite our best efforts to pollute the stream to death. Pick a rock up, and you're likely to see half a dozen multilegged creatures scuttling from the sun, various larvae, mostly may- and stonefly, an occasional, larger dragonfly, sometimes a full-grown water penny or, find of find, a pincer-waving hellgrammite big enough to scare a boy into dropping the rock he's found it beneath. Safer and commoner is the crawdad, betrayed by the bright-colored pebbles scattered in front of its entrance, backpedaling away, with Edward in pursuit.

Feet dried, beer drunk, crawdads fled, we pile back in our canoe and float downstream again, the river carrying us four miles an hour toward home. "Rapids, Daddy, rapids" shakes my lethargy from time to time, and we paddle thirty frantic seconds, whooping and hollering as the canoe, bottom be damned, bounces from rock to rock, shipping water, and Edward sure we're dead at any moment, perhaps this very moment, what with rock here and there and everywhere, and now I'm wide awake and threading our way between huge, uneroded chunks of Virginia smeared with canoe paint, and pulling the boat back from that jagged behemoth rearing up just there, and dodging that solid limestone submarine there. And then we find the slot, the water veeing downriver and the channel floating us, and we shoot it like pros. The river just gives up, tiring of us and currents and froth, and falls asleep, its bottom dropping down, down, down to darkness and who knows what. The river is now a dark brown mystery, swallowed trees grasping for light as they drown in its depths, and giant catfish and carp and snapping turtles waiting to snag our toes and haul us down. Then the Maury cheers again, shallows, and flows but three feet deep, her bottom bare limestone bedrock, each crevice a jumble of red and gray and brown and white sandstones carried from Goshen. River grass and weed push up between them, yellow and

View of the North (now Maury)
River. From Edward Pollard, *The
Virginia Tourist* (Philadelphia:
Lippincott, 1870)

white and blue flowers rising just above water- level perches for damsel and
dragonflies, and against the bank, a bark-stripped box elder winks whitely where
a beaver dropped it. Overhead, basswood is heavy with bee-bothered blossoms,
banksides are a florist's window of spice bush, Joe-pye, and jewelweed. That tangle of leaves and sticks snagged in a sycamore crotch ten feet above us is the only
clue that, come winter, the Maury rouses herself and roars, flooding overnight,
scaring beaver, coon, cow, and man to higher ground.

Rather than weekend voyagers, the Maury hosted two hundred years ago
bateauxmen, muscled mountain men hauling furs from the frontier to Richmond
and beyond. Then Cedar Creek, but three weekend cabins today, was Grand Central for fur traders coming east out of the mountains, the stone foundations of
house and wall still visible in the scruffy woods leading down to the river. Here
where Goshen Pass's rocks died away and the Maury deepened enough for boats,
they piled their furs aboard wooden bateaux and waited for the river to rise. Then
they ran her, whooping and hollering, far drunker and more skilled than I, and
made a fortune off Allegheny beaver pelt.

Rivers stayed Virginia's highways for nearly a hundred years. Anthony Rucker of Amherst County on the other side of the Blue Ridge even patented a boat designed to carry a dozen thousand-pound hogsheads of tobacco down the James. Thomas Jefferson bought one in 1775, writing, *"Rucker's battoe is 50. f. long. 4.f. wide in the bottom & 6.f. at top. She carries 11. hhds & draws 13½ I. water."* The Maury, though, was the etiolated tip of river traffic, long, narrow, shallow, her upper reaches never fully tamed. Below Lexington the North River Navigation Company tied into the James River and Kanahwa Canal so that the lower half of the river was a series of lakes well into the twentieth century. Remnants of dam and lock and towpath line the river, affording picnic spots with ruins so picturesque you squint and think yourself in Europe. Down where South River joins the Maury, they built a bypass canal, gone now save for the massive locks that joined it to the Maury. The locks are now a tree-hung wall of stone that just might be—no, is—a castle wall if you're young enough in fact or mind to think it so, with the river's shaggy cliffs rising hugely behind it, and the Blue Ridge off in the distance, and cows and bees and you the only things enjoying the field that slopes down to the river's edge and is covered with water cress and mint and wild oregano. The railroad soon outdid the canal, stealing its towpath for tracks. And then the railroad too died, washed out by flood after flood, abandoned in 1969. A footpath now follows the railroad's route along the Maury, joggers and hikers using what once carried steam locomotives and boat-towing mules. In spring, the lockkeepers' daffodils, yucca, and periwinkle doggedly bloom on, while out in the river the dams, long since blown up, collapse into a rocky rubble affording canoeists momentary pleasure.

Above Lexington the Maury is still water for nearly a mile, her waters backed up for the moment by the old Lexington Mills Dam at Jordan's Point, though there's talk of tearing it down. For now, though, the still water makes for a dull finish to the river's whiter upper reaches, and most people take out two miles above town where the road crosses the river. That leaves two miles for tubing, a cheap alternative to renting or buying a canoe, with a brand new truck tube only fifteen bucks, and the tire stores in town willing to pump it up for free. Add a beer-filled cooler, and you're set for an afternoon's slow float. Now you feel the full mystery of the Maury's dark pools, floating butt down and feet trolling in water that must have a bottom, though you're damned if you're brave enough to dive and find it. Snorkeling this stretch of river, I've scared myself when the drowned hands of a sycamore tree reached out to grab me. But the mask is worth the fright, revealing six-foot-tall, sky-reaching forests of lime-encrusted chara algae and the oval nests of breeding bluegill, each attended by an anxious male fish, darting out to chase off interlopers, flicking his tail and fluttering his gills to attract the picky, passing females. Here too, Whistle Creek cascades down a limestone staircase that arches its back in a grand curving anticline, its treads pocked with holes worn by cobbles swirling round and down, its rock walls hung with fossil brachiopods and cephalopods, swallows' mud nests hanging from cave entrances overlooking a secret pool, and moss, fern, and liverwort greening the run up to the ruined wall of a long-lost mill.

Downstream, a breached milldam provides a moment's thrill, and then you're floating by a six-foot wall of laid stone, Furr's millrace cut through solid limestone. If you tie up, you can walk his now-dry canal, hunting for trilobites in the carefully set stones that tree and flood are dismantling year by year. In spring, wake robin, trillium, Dutchman's britches, dog's tooth violets, Virginia bluebells, and wild ginger lure you up the shaded hillside. People used to sneak down to the river here and swim on the sandbank on the far side, but a mcmansion sprang up ten years ago, and now a wrecked concrete dock discourages visitors.

But, downstream, ropes still dangle from sycamore after sycamore, daring you to clamber up and grab the graying, frayed, about-to-bust rope and swing out ever so high above the water and let go in a scream of horrible delight and fall, fall, fall, and live. Lexington is announced by the field across the road, filled with cattle when I first tubed this river but now sprouting house after house with the flood plain blooming houses on sticks, and by the dull hum of tire against asphalt.

Some things improve, however, and Jordan's Point is one. Named after the entrepreneur who helped bring the canal to Lexington and who built his house atop the nearby hill to overlook his work and declare it good, Jordan's Point was once terminus for the North River Canal and chockablock with warehouses. The railroad, whose abandoned trestle still stands in ruin where it crosses the narrow creek that makes Jordan's Point an island, decreed the warehouses' demise, and a sewer plant arose to take their place. Built in a floodplain, it shut down with every river-rising rain, and Lexington pumped untreated sewage into the Maury.

The sewer plant is gone from Jordan's Point now; it has been rebuilt bigger and better to handle more development and has been placed where only Noah's Flood can reach it. Where once you waded ashore to the stench of human waste, now you pull up to a graveled incline that leads you, not to offal holding tanks, but to a soccer field.

The point itself is a park, and Edward and I walk there sometimes, lured by the river, which narrows here, picking up speed and so providing a perfect sluiceway for stick-and-leaf races whose finish line lies somewhere beyond the thick piers of Highway 11, crossing here where, two hundred years ago, a rutted wagon way followed the Indian and buffalo trail across the river, dictating that, whatever they named it, the town that sprang up would spring up here. Though the river flows on, here we stop, on the downstream tip of Jordan's Point, its sand bluff sluffing into the river, tugging so at us that we turn back with reluctance, shoulders sore from paddling canoe or tube, but souls refreshed.

⑅ HAY BALES

I have been in love with hay bales, square and round, ever since that long-gone summer when I paid the rent baling hay, the clattering baler spitting square bales out in ragged rows up and down and up and down the field, and me heaving bale upon bale on the wagon that tailed behind, and my roommate stacking, the load taller with each field row we completed, friction and luck frustrating the great fall every jolt threatened, skill and pride building under sun and muscle burn.

Twenty summers later, my family helped the farmer renting our fields stack the bank barn behind the house rafter high with fifty-pound square bales, heaving them off the wagon and stacking them, first this way, then that. Row after row rose toward the tin roof thirty feet above us, until the central bay became a hay cathedral, the air thick with motes and sunshafts through which heavy-winged pigeons flapped. Up those walls the boys clambered to wage war with pine cones flung from hay-bale fort to hay-bale fort and to shelter in sagging-roofed mansions. Their walls were thick with the rustle of field mouse and pursuing black snake, the wild cat's litter of six tumbling in the tangle of bale twine in a cobwebby corner, and the barn swallows' nests stuck like bubble gum to the rough-hewn barn posts. With the rope hung from the highest beam, the boys flung themselves out into air, tarzaning from hay wall to hay wall, arcs growing longer through the winter as, tier- by-tier, we took the bales and flung them down the chute to the cattle below. By spring the grassy ramparts were broken and shattered, and the thick-with-broken-hay-bales barn floor softer than the mattresses the whole family forsook to spend the night in the barn, its doors thrown open to a moon as yellow as the grass we lay upon.

In the trenches of World War I, Robert Bridges remembered "digging tunnels through the hay / In the Big Barn, 'cause it's a rainy day. / Oh springy hay, and lovely beams to climb! / You're back in the old sailor suit again. / It's a queer time." And though, thank God, we've been spared that squandering of a generation's youth, we all have memories stored up in memory's barns, like so many sweet-breathed summer-cut flowers, timothy orchard and rye grass, red and white clover, violets and knap weed and mullein, so that when, stuck like cows in nursing homes, we might burp up happier times and chew our memories' cuds. Even cattle, starved for sun and greenery come winter, feed on summer's memories, the giant bales taken to fields worn brown and bare and let roll downhill in long-lined cafeterias, spilling onto the ground from which they rose the grasses from which the flesh we eat is grown.

Too old for war and haying, I've a more philosophic rapport with bales. Summer evenings hiking the valley's back roads, that end-of-the-day lost feeling upon me, legs and back and spirit aching, shadows rising from field and ditch, nowhere to lay my head, farmhouse dogs barking meanly, no vacant wood to hide in, I top a hill, and there they graze. A herd of great-backed round bales rises shaggy as buffalo from a darkening field rich with the promise of sweet-scented shelter as the sky fills with stars. And, wrapped in a summer blanket, snuggled up against the warm flank of a breeze-blocking bale, whiskey in hand, I am the only person to hear the coyotes wailing on North Mountain.

Before the tractor and its scissor-clattering sickle bar and baler, haying was a tranquil task, as Robert Frost remembered, with "never a sound beside the wood but one, / And that was my long scythe whispering to the ground." Today it's the wind through the field before it's hayed that brings such whispering to mind, the same whispers of death, beautiful death that Walt Whitman heard in the sibilant surf on Long Island, that poetic-minded artists from Andrew Marvell to Winslow Homer heard as they wrote about or painted mowers playing Death himself in summer's fields, everyone then knowing "all flesh is grass," as the Bible has it.

Dried in the sun, the scythe-slain grass and flowers were turned by tedders, men and women with forks and rakes, who'd mound the hay in windrows later stacked in the fields or piled on wagons and carted off to sheltering barns. Old valley farms still have shorter and longer handled pitchforks designed to replace each other as the piles grew taller and taller. Stacking such hay required skill, Frost remembers in "Death of the Hired Man," where Warren compliments Silas by remarking, "He bundles every forkful in its place, / And tags and numbers it for future reference, / So he can find and easily dislodge it / In the unloading. Silas does that well. / He takes it out in bunches like big birds' nests. / You never see him standing on the hay / He's trying to lift, straining to lift himself." Weather might ruin the downward sloping outer layer of hay on stacks left in the field, but inside the hay stayed edible, as you can tell by looking closely at a round bale you chance upon.

Young bodies that spent long days together pitching hay often spent more pleasant hours in pursuit of other pleasures in the shelter of the hay they'd stacked. As English Romantic poet Thomas Hood declared, "Oh! there's nothing in life like making love, / Save making hay in fine weather!" From eighteenth-century

Hay Bales in Rockbridge County, by Alice Ireland. Collection of the artist

France's Jean-Honoré Fragonard to nineteenth-century America's Winslow Homer to twentieth-century Hollywood's Jane Russell, haying has been the backdrop for sexual dalliance and the staining of brocades and honor. Generations of bored English literature students have perked up at Robert Herrick's "Many a green-gown has been given; / Many a kiss, both odd and even: / Many a glance, too, has been sent / From out the eye, love's firmament: / Many a jest told of the keys betraying / This night, and locks pick'd:—yet we're not a Maying," the gown greened from a roll in the grass or new-mown hay.

Hay is grass complete with seed heads, cut while still green. Straw is leftover stalks after grain—corn, wheat, oats, barley, rice—has been harvested in the fall. Both are cut using machines that valley native Cyrus McCormick helped develop. Preserved by the state, McCormick's childhood farm lies just over the border in Augusta County, where a twenty-two-year-old McCormick built in six weeks in 1831 a reaper that revolutionized farming and made him world famous and wealthy. Before McCormick, grain was cut with a cradle, a scythe outfitted with a frame of four wooden fingers that allowed the reaper to cut the grain and throw it in a swath, where it lay until raked. Two acres was considered a good day's work. McCormick's two-person mechanical reaper cut six times as much, as a local farmer testified in the Lexington newspaper in the summer of 1833: "I have seen Mr. Cyrus H. McCormick's grain cutting machine in operation for two seasons. It cut for me this season—I think it will perform well where the ground is free of rocks and stumps; and will be a great saving over hand labor and can be so constructed as to cut much wider than at present, and I think it well worth the attention of the public. I think it will cut about 12 acres per day by being well attended."

Rockbridge County's rocky and stumpy fields were ill made for such a machine, however, and McCormick headed west to Chicago and the Great Plains, whose vast fields his machines conquered, Abraham Lincoln's secretary of state, William H. Seward, proclaiming in 1860 that, thanks to McCormick's invention, "the line of civilization moves westward thirty miles each year." At first McCormick's reaper merely cut the crop more efficiently than scythes could. But the ever-inventive McCormick added a binder to tie the cut grain in sheaves, and later a thresher. Hayers soon adapted the McCormick reaper to haying as well, with the result that one-man tractor-drawn hay balers crisscross fields that once required a dozen workers a week to hay.

As McCormick's fame and fortunes rose, so too did controversy, as others claimed their reapers were earlier or better. My college library has the legacy of one such controversy, Follett Greeno's lengthily titled *Obed Hussey, Who, of All Inventors, Made Bread Cheap; Being a True Record of His Life and Struggles to Introduce His Greatest Invention, the Reaper, and Its Success, as Gathered from Pamphlets Published Heretofore by Some of His Friends and Associates, and Reprinted in this Volume, Together with Some Additional Facts and Testimonials from Other Sources* and R. B. Swift's shorter titled *Who Invented the Reaper? An Answer to the Protest Statement Said to Have Been Filed at the Treasury Department.* Hussey's reaper was nearly McCormick's twin, being but two years younger. Anyway, priority was less the key to McCormick's success than business savvy, which involved him in tussles with other reaper manufacturers and workers. Two years after his death, workers at his Chicago McCormick Harvesting Machine Company striking for an eight-hour workday were shot by police, precipitating the next day's Haymarket Affair, in which eight police and no one knows how many workers were killed in a riot after someone threw a bomb. Playing up the public's fear, the government executed four anarchists, none of whom had thrown the bomb. To this day, many nations remember the riot by celebrating International Workers' Day on May 1, the day the strike for an eight-hour workday began. But not America, whose September date for Labor Day President Grover Cleveland picked as an alternative to the politically volatile May 1 following his sending twelve thousand troops to suppress Eugene V. Debs's 1894 strike against George Pullman's railroad sleeping-car company.

Such industrial strife seems far removed from the hay bales in whose shade I rest. Even these may be doomed. Left long in the fields, they are apt to be ingested by giant white worms, fifteen or twenty bales long, that crawl to the field's edge and rest the fall and winter through, gorged and white as fish bellies. These are the latest way to make silage out of new-mown hay, wrapping it, still green, in thick white plastic that swells like a plump tick as the hay within ferments. Unpretty but utilitarian. And the bane of Celia, who makes her living painting Rockbridge County's hay bales for people like me to hang upon their walls and dream of summer through the long dark winters of our discontent.

SEXUAL SWARMS

The fraternities two blocks away are at their mating rituals again, mind-numbingly loud music syncopating with choruses of drunken screams of delight as groups of khaki-panted, polo-shirted look-alikes seduce giggling sorority girls with their puking antics. Birds do it, bees do it, we do it: sexual swarming, groups of males strutting their stuff before females, who pick and choose with whom to mate according to barely understood and often bizarre-seeming sexual algorithms.

Tens of thousands of ants swarmed on our lawn on hot days in late summer. The air was thick and still, the ants fragile, white wings bright against their dark bodies as they clambered out of subterranean tunnels I'd not even suspected lay beneath the grass. Leaders were pressed by following hordes to the top of grass blades and then into the air, where they flew in clotted clouds of fornicating formicans, landing upon my arms, my legs, my face, too intent on sex to bother biting. Nuptial flights, the bug people call these magic moments when fertile females, picking from among a thousand anxious males, store up sperm for a life-time of laying eggs beneath the earth. Sated with sex, they tear their wings off, becoming matrons. The males, off course, live hard, die young, and, if they're lucky, enjoy a brief fuck in the sky, before falling back to earth, a thousand thou-sand winged corpses littering the grass from whence they came, as their lovers, already forgetting their dying mates, fly off to never-never land.

Well, who hasn't felt at times like a forsaken formican, haunted by those whom we love leaving with someone else, our wings heavy with disappointment and defeat? Older, lonelier, less hopeful, more calloused, I listen to the night howls of frat boys learning love's hard lessons.

Autumn, and John Keats and I overhear, "in a wailful choir, the small gnats mourn / Among the river sallows, borne aloft / Or sinking as the light wind lives or dies." Not mourning, at least not wittingly, these insects, mainly midges, jig up and down in mid air, forming faint clouds that I collide with on my jogs, gnats sticking to my wet face, and my coughing up and crunching the two or three invariably sucked down my windpipe. They're mostly males, gathered together here over this sunny spot or cow's rump to mate with whatever female they can convince to join them. Just what makes one bug desirable to another remains obscure to human observers, but to that something, dying generations of midge, mosquito, and gnat testify.

Biologists call these dancing clouds *leks*, from the Swedish word for play, kin to the noun in our *out on a lark*. To biologists, leks are gatherings of males for competitive mating displays. America's most famous examples are our sage grouse and prairie chickens, which gather together for strutting and booming displays on the prairies. The extinct heath hen, which once boomed and strutted in leks from Maine south to Virginia's Eastern Shore, was driven to extinction in 1932, a fate we seem determined to inflict upon its Great Plains cousins as well. Unable, then, to watch these birds, I must content myself with Audubon's enthusiastic description of those he saw in Kentucky: "Imagine them assembled, to the number of twenty, by day-break, see them all strutting in the presence of each other, mark their consequential gestures, their looks of disdain, and their angry pride, as they pass each other. Their tails are spread out and inclined forwards, to meet the expanded feathers of their neck, which now, like stiffened frills, lie supported by the globular orange-coloured receptacles of air, from which their singular booming sounds proceed.... Like Game Cocks they strike, and rise in the air to meet their assailants with greater advantage. Now many close in the encounter; feathers are seen whirling in the agitated air, or falling around them tinged with blood. The weaker begin to give way, and one after another seek refuge in the neighbouring bushes. The remaining few, greatly exhausted, maintain their ground, and withdraw slowly and proudly, as if each claimed the honours of victory. The vanquished and the victors then search for the females, who, believing each to have returned from the field in triumph, receive them with joy." Even in Audubon's day, their numbers were diminishing, and he wrote that they had "abandoned the State of Kentucky, and removed (like the Indians) every season farther to the westward, to escape from the murderous white man." Not west enough, though, and they, and the Carolina parakeet, the passenger pigeon, the Labrador duck, the great auk, and Eskimo curlew have all flown into the abyss that awaits us all, lek though we might for mates to parent progeny.

Every summer, mayflies desperate to reproduce shroud the lights along the East Lexington bridge in an orgy of copulation. These are the winged grownups whose feathery-gilled juveniles Edward scares up under river rocks where they scavenge the detritus for one to two years before ascending to the surface, splitting their nymphal exoskeleton, and flying off, unless fed on by fish, which so delight in them that trout fishermen make imitation mayfly flies. Should they survive the fish and the bat and dragonfly gauntlet waiting above, male mayflies swarm by the thousands, dancing up and down in a thick cloud over the river, waiting for females to fly in and mate with them. Mayflies were famous in the nineteenth century as "the only genus of winged insect that never sees the sun"; they earned the name *ephemera*, creatures of a day, most adults living less than twenty four hours. Some people called them insects of an hour, and it was of mayflies that Keats could have written, "when I feel, fair creature of an hour, / That I shall never look upon thee more," though in fact he was remembering an anonymous woman he saw in a public garden in London. Like him, who of us hasn't mourned an unknown beauty from afar, chagrined that we should never know or see her again? Think then how it must be to be a mayfly, born to die so quickly that you don't even have a mouth to eat with or to woo or kiss your lover with, condemned to anonymous sex and death by drowning.

This fate may be no worse than what awaits some male fireflies in our backyards. Famous for their nightly pyromania, our summer fireflies are almost all males, all winking at females, who respond with their own wink, wink, nudge, nudge come-hithers carefully attuned to the blinking pattern ordained them by Mother Nature. The *Photuris* females wink, wink, nudge, nudge to male *Photinus* fireflies, then eat those foolish enough to fly by for a rendezvous. These *femmes fatales* get not only protein from their hapless, horny prey, but also a predator-repellant chemical. Reason enough for this behavior, one supposes, and not that far removed from certain human females' seeking money and a predator-repellant gold ring. One *Photuris* species seduces eleven different kinds of fireflies, and at least one battered *Photinus* species has six different predators, all of which puts *Looking For Mr. Goodbar* in perspective. But it's what inspired *Photuris* cannibalism that interests us here: synchronous flashing. Southeast Asian fireflies are famous for lighting up riverfront trees at the same time, Sir Francis Drake having described them as long ago as 1577: "Amongst these Trees, night by night, through the whole Land, did shew themselves an infinite swarme of fierie Wormes flying in the Ayre, whose bodies being no bigger than common English Flyes, make such a shew and light, as if every Twigge or Tree had beene a burning Candle." No scientist knew, until a few years ago, that fireflies in Tennessee's Smoky Mountains also synchronize. Scattered populations of synchronizing fireflies have since been found up and down the Appalachians, as far west as Texas, and on the Georgia coast. And I'm no scientist, but I could swear my backyard fireflies blink on and off in temporary unison, though that may be wine talking. Such synchronicity, some savants surmise, is but a relic of a once far more common synchronous swarming, made scarce when hungry *Photuris* fireflies homed in on the fireworks, so that, today, North American fireflies can flash together only where there are few if any waiting *Photuris*. Summer nights when the fraternities are howling at the moon and I cannot sleep, I watch from my upstairs window the fireflies blinking on and off, rising higher as the night deepens, ever more desperate in their quests to mate, ever more reckless in the come-hither winks they respond to. They are not unlike either my younger self or those still unmated hooligans whose taste in music is deplorable.

Not that we can be picky when it comes to lekking—or disliking—where we gather for sex. Though land-dwelling, amphibians return to water to mate, often in nearly frightening numbers, so that valley wet bars can be a cacophony of horny males yelling "Pick me, pick me, pick me." For years I lived in a farmhouse built beside a small spring rising from beneath a rocky ledge that ran downhill for a hundred feet until it sank underground again, not to reappear for a dry quarter of mile. Somehow, a bullfrog had made his way there, and spring and summer he spent his nights knee-deep, knee-deeping for a woman who never came, much like those two-legged amphibia swimming in spilt beer down the street. This late at night I want to yell, "No self-respecting woman's going home with you. Turn off the music and go to bed." Neither the fratty baggers nor the bullfrog pays attention, so I am condemned to wander my empty house, listening to their ever-more-desperate choruses and wondering why I too am bedding down alone.

We males are desperate creatures, dry hollows and womanless parties but two of the many obstacles we face. Early spring, and salamanders and I begin our yearly search for mates. Like me, they have their favorite watering holes, muddy versions of the bars I've sought Sallies in. Just off the Blue Ridge Parkway, the Appalachian Trail's Punchbowl shelter sits near a small, spring-fed pool filled in March with thick-tailed female salamanders swarmed over by smaller males desperate to mate, so jostling each other you wonder how anyone manages to do anything. Nearer town, on Brushy Hill, the road is littered on wet spring mornings with squashed carcasses as the hellbent-on-mating salamanders make their way to a cattail-choked pond, where newts hang tail down in the water awaiting company. Up on North Mountain, their cousins congregate in a muddy sump a thousand feet higher and half a mile away from any other water source that yet is home sweet home to scores of salamanders that, science tells us, can scent their ways back to their natal waters. These are all red-spotted newts, which begin life as greenish-brown tadpoles with gills, metamorphosing by summer's end into spotted, reddish-orange, terrestrial-dwelling efts for two to three years before reverting to olive-green, aquatic adults. Ancient and unglaciated, the southern Appalachians are a hotbed of salamander diversity, and the nearby Peaks of Otter harbor their own particular species, though it's hard to say from photographs whether the newts I saw lining the pond at the Peaks were these or some less notable species. But swarming they were, large, fat-tailed newts every few feet along the pond's edge, sluggish in the still cold water, and, cold-blooded though they be, hearts warming to the thought of slimy sex.

Closer to home, even the fish taunt old men like me, sunfish lining the Maury and the farm ponds I sneak a peak at with their come-hither spawning nests, two to three feet across, bowl-shaped depressions cleared out with tail and mouth, grouped together like whore houses outside a military base. Back and forth and round and round the males swim, obsessively sweeping their floors and chasing off interlopers, hoping hope against fishy hope that a female will swim up from the depths so that they might rush out and entice her back to the nest, there to mingle milt and eggs that the father will care for. Among those young may be another's children, though, since some males specialize, not in building nests, but in cuckolding those who do build them. These "cuckold males" dart in, mingle their milt with the nest builder's, and leave, letting another raise their young. Yet other males are female mimics, imitating female sunfish so that, when they sidle up to a copulating couple, the male ignores them.

In the sky above, male green darner dragonflies are as busily patrolling as are the fish below. Back and forth, back and forth they fly along that section of the pond bank they have chosen as their own, constantly on the lookout for interlopers. Sitting in the shade, I watch them through binoculars, listening for the dry rattle of wings as they fight for possession of thirty feet of mud and weeds, two males grappling in midair, tussling, the interloper, often as not, flying off while the victor continues his relentless border patrols. To his left and right fly other males, the pond bank one mating station after another. But to a passing female, this or that to us unremarkable stretch of mud bespeaks her wooer's genetic fitness, and should she find this clump here of pondweed and algae to her liking, she'll let its possessor grab her head and fly her to the moon. Having lost the dragonfly of their dreams, lesser darners dart back and forth, back and forth, barely swiveling their 360-degree gazing heads to watch what they would but cannot do: clasp her to themselves in a flying wheel, head to tail and tail to head, and never let her go until she's laid their eggs. And then it's back to patrolling once again; who knows, perhaps another big-eyed beauty will pass this way.

"That is no country for old men. The young / in one another's arms, . . ." Yeats had Byzantium, but I am stuck with Lexington, Virginia. Where are my leks? Several years ago, when I told Edward we would go to church in a move to find a woman, he sagely answered, "But, Daddy, you wouldn't get along with the kind of women who go to church." Nor does bar-hopping at fifty-seven lure me. And I've never found the local grocery's veggie section prime lekking ground. But the Balls invited me to Daisy's wedding, which took place on a rainy summer's day when everyone crowded together under the porch, and I met Celia, fetching in her clingy, damp dress, who thought me rumpled but perhaps more possible than the other aging men who hit upon her. Funerals and marriages, I explain to my literature students, are excellent lekking grounds. They don't listen, of course, so I must listen to them, their music louder and louder as the night grows later and later and the prospects dimmer and dimmer, dancing the dance that midges, ants, mayflies, fireflies, bullfrogs, newts, birds, and dragonflies dance, that we all dance, or would dance, were nature kinder and women more generous.

Notes

I include each chapter's major sources. Where possible I have listed internet links.

Sugar Creek

Geological information on karst can be found in a lengthy article posted by the United States Department of the Interior, "Engineering Aspects of Karst" in *National Atlas of the United States,* http://www.nationalatlas.gov/articles/geology/a__karst.html (accessed November 7, 2009). The shorter *Karst: Virginia Natural Heritage Karst Program,* Cave and Karst Protection, Virginia Department of Conservation and Recreation, appears online at http://www.dcr.virginia.gov (accessed November 7, 2009). Charles A. Grymes discusses "Wind Gaps and Stream Piracy," at *Virginia Places,* http://www.virginiaplaces.org/ (accessed November 7, 2009).

Rock Crystals

The geology department of William and Mary provides a detailed look of the state's geology in "The Geology of Virginia," online at http://web.wm.edu/geology/Virginia (accessed November 7, 2009). Richard Stoiber, Carl Tolman, and Robert Butler give an overview of the importance of quartz crystals during World War II. Their "Geology of Quartz Crystal Deposits" appears in *American Mineralogist* 30 (May 1945), online at http://www.minsocam.org/msa/collectors__corner/amtoc/toc1945.htm (accessed November 7, 2009).

The Shenandoah Sea

Many editions of Thomas Jefferson's 1781 *Notes on the State of Virginia* exist, including one online at http://etext.virginia.edu/toc/modeng/public/JefVirg.html (accessed November 7, 2009). The geology department of the College of William and Mary provides a detailed look at the state's geology in "The Geology of Virginia," http://web.wm.edu/geology/Virginia (accessed November 7, 2009). Keith Frye's *The Roadside Geology of Virginia* (Missoula, Mt.: Mountain Press Publishing Company, 1986) is a portable guide to rock formations you can see from your car. Founded by Young Earth Creationist Henry M. Morris, the Museum of Creation and Earth History in California, online at http://www.lifeandlightfoundation.org (accessed November 7, 2009), and Kentucky's more recent Creation Museum, http://www.creationmuseum.org (accessed November 7, 2009), both argue for a literal interpretation of Genesis. Morris is co-author with John Whitcomb of *The Genesis Flood: The Biblical Record and Its Scientific Implications* (Phillipsburg, N.J.: Presbyterian & Reformed Publishing, 1961), a Creationist text popular with

Fundamentalist Christians. Ronald L. Numbers's *The Creationists: From Scientific Creationism to Intelligent Design* (Cambridge: Harvard University Press, 2006) is an academic examination of the history of antievolutionary thought.

Caves

Geological information on karst can be found in a lengthy article posted by the United States Department of the Interior, "Engineering Aspects of Karst" in *National Atlas of the United States*, http://www.nationalatlas.gov/articles/geology/a__karst.html (accessed November 7, 2009). The shorter *Karst: Virginia Natural Heritage Karst Program*, Cave and Karst Protection, Virginia Department of Conservation and Recreation, appears at http://www.dcr.virginia.gov (accessed November 7, 2009). The *National Karst Map*, an ongoing project by, among others, the U.S. Geological Survey and the U.S. Fish and Wildlife Service also discusses karst topography, online at http://www.nature.nps.gov/nckri/map/project/index.html (accessed November 7, 2009). Both the Rockbridge County cave planarian (*Sphalloplana virginiana*) and the Rockbridge County cave amphipod (*Stygobromus baroodyi*) are of concern to the U.S. Fish and Wildlife Service, according to *Threatened, Endangered, and Special Concern Aquatic Species*, an online study of the Southern Appalachian Cooperative Ecosystem Studies Unit, at http://cesu.utk.edu/documents/ (accessed November 7, 2009).

Rock Castles

The Division of Geology and Mineral Resources publishes geological maps and booklets detailing the geology of individual counties and quadrants within counties, including K. F. Bick, *Geology of the Lexington Quadrangle, Virginia* (Charlottesville: Division of Mineral Resources, 1960); S. J. Kozak, *Geology of the Millboro Quadrangle, Virginia* (Charlottesville: Division of Mineral Resources, 1965); and Gerald P. Wilkes, Edgar W. Spencer, Nick H. Evans, and Elizabeth V. M. Campbell, *Geology of Rockbridge County, Virginia* (Charlottesville: Division of Mineral Resources, 1977). A discussion of Ice Age talus slopes visible from the interstate appears in *Glimpses of the Ice Age from I-81*, Geologic Wonders of the George Washington and Jefferson National Forests, No. 1 in a series, Lee Ranger District, U.S. Department of Interior, U.S. Geological Survey, U.S. Department of Agriculture Forest Service, Southern Region, 1998, http://pubs.usgs.gov/gip/ (accessed November 7, 2009).

The Natural Bridge

Many editions of Thomas Jefferson's 1781 *Notes on the State of Virginia* exist, including one online at http://etext.virginia.edu/toc/modeng/public/JefVirg.html (accessed November 7, 2009). The Natural Bridge Web site, http://www.naturalbridgeva.com/bridge.html (accessed November 7, 2009), has descriptions of its various attractions. Gilmer's natural explanation is quoted in *The Height of Our Mountains: Nature Writing from Virginia's Blue Ridge Mountains and Shenandoah Valley* (Baltimore: Johns Hopkins University Press, 1998), edited by Michael P. Branch and Daniel J. Philippon. David Hunter Strother's *Virginia Illustrated* (New York: Harper, 1871) contains the amusing and informative sketches of nineteenth-century Virginia by Strother (better known as Porte

Crayon), including his account of stopping on the bridge with his horrified cousin, online at http://books.google.com (accessed November 7, 2009). François-René de Chateaubriand's international best-selling 1801 novel *Atala* and its 1802 sequel *René* prominently feature the Natural Bridge. Herman Melville mentions the bridge in "The Chase, the First Day," in *Moby-Dick* (1851). Frank Holt discusses Hicks's use of the bridge in his review of the Williamsburg, Virginia, Abby Aldrich Rockefeller Folk Art Center's show on Hicks; Holt's "The Kingdoms of Edward Hicks" appears in *Folk Art Messenger* 12 (Spring 1999), online at http://www.folkart.org/ (accessed November 7, 2009). You can read about and see pictures of the French wallpaper featuring the bridge, which now graces the walls of the Diplomatic Reception Room at the White House, online at http://www.whitehousemuseum.org/floor0/diplomatic-room.htm (accessed November 7, 2009). On March 24, 1873, the *New York Times* reported the bridge's burning but the next day repudiated the story as a publicity stunt. Edmund Burke's 1757 *Philosophical Enquiry into the Origin of our Ideas of the Sublime and Beautiful* is available online in many editions, including that at http://www.bartleby.com/24/2/ (accessed November 7, 2009). Washington and Lee professor Edgar Spencer discusses geological history in "Natural Bridge and Vicinity," *Virginia Minerals* 10 (May 1964), online at http://www.dmme.virginia.gov/ (accessed November 7, 2009). Bonner R. Cohen explains the absence of crass commercialism at the bridge in his article "Private Conservation: An Environmental Success Story" (Heartland Institute), online at http://www.heartland.org/ (accessed November 7, 2009).

Stone Walls

James H. Wood, *The War: "Stonewall" Jackson, His Campaigns and Battles, the Regiment as I Saw Them* (Cumberland, Md.: Eddy Press, 1910), online at http://www.archive.org/index.php (accessed November 7, 2009), describes the VMI cadets' encounter with the House Mountain Men. The 1860 U.S. Census, available online from the U.S. Census Bureau at http://www.census.gov/prod/www/abs/decennial/1860.htm (accessed November 7, 2009), gives population figures by race for states, counties, and cities. Susan Allport's *Sermons in Stone: The Stone Walls of New England and New York* (New York: Norton, 1994) is but one of several books that discuss the art of building various kinds of dry stone walls. Rockbridge geology is described in several of Virginia's Division of Geology and Mineral Resources geological reports, including K. F. Bick's *Geology of the Lexington Quadrangle, Virginia* (Charlottesville: Division of Mineral Resources, 1960), S. J. Kozak's *Geology of the Millboro Quadrangle, Virginia* (Charlottesville: Division of Mineral Resources, 1965), and Gerald P. Wilkes, Edgar W. Spencer, Nick H. Evans, and Elizabeth V. M. Campbell's *Geology of Rockbridge County, Virginia* (Charlottesville: Division of Mineral Resources, 1977). The wall the House Mountain men built alludes to Nehemiah in the Old Testament and Robert Frost's "Mending Wall."

Geological Segregation

Eric Gorton wrote about Goshen's origins in "Building a Bridge from Yesteryear," in the U.S. Department of Transportation's *Public Roads* 67 (January–February 2004), online at http://www.tfhrc.gov/pubrds/04jan/07.htm (accessed November 7, 2009). Lynda

Mundy-Norris Miller's history of Glasgow, *One Hundred Years of Dreams* (Berryville, Va.: Rockbridge Publishing,1992), is excerpted on the Glasgow town Web site, http://www.glasgowvirginia.org/ (accessed November 7, 2009). Oren Frederic Morton discusses early real-estate quarrels as well as the booms and busts of Buena Vista, Glasgow, and Goshen in his *A History of Rockbridge County, Virginia* (Staunton, Va. McClure, 1920), online at http://books.google.com/ (accessed November 7, 2009). The 1860 U.S. Census, available online from the U.S. Census Bureau at http://www.census .gov/prod/www/abs/decennial/1860.htm (accessed November 7, 2009), gives population figures by race for states, counties, and cities. Descriptions of local floods are posted online by the Virginia Department of Emergency Management, http://www.vdem.state .va.us/library/plans/ (accessed November 7, 2009). The U.S. Forest Service brochure on St. Mary Wilderness is online at http://www.fs.fed.us/r8/gwj/gp/pdf__files/saint-mary's .pdf (accessed November 7, 2009).

Massanutten

John Fontaine recounted Governor Spottswood's discovery of the Shenandoah Valley in his journal, included in Ann Maury's *Memoirs of a Huguenot Family* (New York: Putnam, 1872), online at http://books.google.com/ (accessed November 7, 2009). The Hotchkiss Map Collection at the Library of Congress can be viewed online at http://lcweb2 .loc.gov/ammem/collections/maps/hotchkiss/ (accessed November 7, 2009). James I. Robertson Jr.'s *Stonewall in the Shenandoah: The Valley Campaign of* 1862 (Gettysburg: Historical Times, 1972) details the Valley Campaign. An overview is provided by Paul Christopher Anderson's "Shenandoah Valley during the Civil War," in *The Encyclopedia Virginia* (Virginia Foundation for the Humanities), online at http://www.encyclopedi-avirginia.org/ (accessed November 7, 2009). The Virginia Military Institute's Preston Library Archives have primary documents describing Hunter's raid, online at http://www.vmi.edu/ (accessed November 7, 2009). Scott C. Patchan, *Shenandoah Summer: The 1864 Valley Campaign* (Lincoln: University of Nebraska Press, 2007), describes McCausland's burning of Chambersburg.

Forest Communities

Paul A. Colinvaux discusses Clements in "The Nation States of Trees," in his extremely readable *Why Big Fierce Animals Are Rare: An Ecologist's Perspective* (Princeton: Princeton University Press, 1979), online at http://books.google.com (accessed November 7, 2009). You can visit relic Ice Age communities in West Virginia's Cranberry Glades Botanical Area of the Monongahela National Forest, or their electronic equivalent at their Web site, http://www.fs.fed.us/r9/mnf/sp/cranberry__glades.html (accessed November 7, 2009). The National Park Service's "Forest Vegetation Monitoring" fact sheet lists several threats to the Shenandoah National Park, as does the U.S. Geological Survey's "Acid Rain in Shenandoah National Park, Virginia" fact sheet, both online at http://www.nps.gov/shen/ (accessed November 7, 2009).

Cedars

U.S. Supreme Court, *Miller v. Schoene*, 276 U.S. 272 (1928) decided for apple growers over cedar lovers, online at http://supreme.justia.com/us/276/272/case.html (accessed November 7, 2009). The *New York Times* covered both the Virginia and West Virginia controversies. William Fischel analyzes the background to and coverage of Serena Dandridge's cedar-tree protest in "The Law and Economics of Cedar-Apple Rust: State Action and Just Compensation in Miller v. Schoene," Dartmouth College Economics Working Paper (February 2005), available online at http://ssrn.com/abstract=524982 (accessed November 7, 2009). Alexander's fire observation is quoted in James Waddel Alexander's *The Life of Archibald Alexander* (New York: Scribner, 1854).

Maple Syrup

John Lawson, an ill-fated colonial explorer whom the Indians burned alive, mentions the sugar maple in his 1718 *A New Voyage to Carolina*, online at http://docsouth.unc.edu (accessed November 7, 2009). Founding Father, friend of presidents, and physician Benjamin Rush in 1791 wrote "An Account of the Sugar Maple Tree" as a letter to Thomas Jefferson; it was reprinted in *Essays Literary, Moral, and Philosophical*, second edition (Philadelphia: Thomas & William Bradford, 1816), online at http://books.google.com (accessed November 7, 2009). Jefferson's maple orchard is mentioned in the "Sugar Maple" entry in the *Thomas Jefferson Encyclopedia*, online at http://wiki.monticello.org (accessed November 7, 2009). Alan Taylor's *William Cooper's Town: Power and Persuasion on the Frontier of the Early American Republic* (New York: Vintage, 1996) details Cooper's failed sugar dreams, while Holland Land Company agent John Lincklaen's *Travels in the Years 1791 and 1792 in Pennsylvania, New York and Vermont*, translated by Helen Lincklaen Fairchild (New York: Putnam, 1897) is online at http://books.google.com (accessed November 7, 2009). Berkeley is quoted in Alice Morse Earle, *Home Life in Colonial Days* (New York: Macmillan, 1898), online at http://books.google.com (accessed November 7, 2009).

Poison Ivy

Donald G. Crosby examines poison ivy and other toxic plants in *The Poisoned Weed* (New York: Oxford University Press, 2004), online at http://www.google.com (accessed November 7, 2009). Peter Hatch mentions Jefferson's growing poison ivy in "Garden Weeds in the Age of Jefferson," *Twinleaf* 18 (2006), online at http://www.twinleaf.org (accessed November 7, 2009). Glenn Winterringer quotes John Smith and others in *Poison-Ivy and Poison-Sumac*, Story of Illinois Series 13 (1963), online at http://www.archive.org/stream/poisonivypoisons13wint (accessed November 7, 2009). Peter Kalm recounts his adventure with poison ivy in his *Travels in North America*, which I read in Adolph B. Benson's 1937 translation, *The America of 1750: Peter Kalm's Travels in North America* (New York, Wilson-Erickson, 1937). Francis Porcher wrote his full-of-trivia 1863 *Resources of the Southern Fields and Forests, Medical, Economical, and Agricultural*, online at http://

docsouth.unc.edu/imls/porcher/porcher.html (accessed November 7, 2009), at the request of the Confederate government to provide alternatives to goods and medicines blockaded by the Union fleet. Several homeopathic texts are available online, including John Henry Clarke's two-volume *A Dictionary of Practical Materia Medica* (London: Homeopathic Publishing, 1902), online at http://books.google.com (accessed November 7, 2009), which discusses Dufresnoy in "Rhus Toxicodendron." Wikipedia is perhaps the quickest place to find a discussion of the relative merits of cures for poison ivy. The "Poison Ivy Cure" appears in *Time Magazine*, October 19, 1942, online at http://www.time.com/time/ (accessed November 7, 2009). Frederick William Beechey writes about California's ubiquitous poison oak in *Narrative of a Voyage to the Pacific and Beering's Strait* (London: Henry Colburn & Richard Bentley, 1831), online at http://books.google.com (accessed November 7, 2009). *A Checklist for the South China Botanical Garden, Guangzhou, Guangdong Province, People's Republic of China,* online at http://www.efloras.org/flora__page.aspx?flora__id=610 (accessed November 7, 2009), states there are sixteen *Toxicodendron* species in China, six endemic.

Sassafras

Charles Lamb related the joys of saloop in "The Praise of Chimney-Sweepers," *The Essays of Elia* (New York: Macmillan, 1909), online at http://books.google.com (accessed November 7, 2009). *The Oxford English Dictionary* provides etymological information on saloop. David L. Cowen quotes both Monardes and Raleigh in "Boom and Bust: Sassafras," *Apothecary's Cabinet* 8 (Fall 2004), online at http://cms.pharmacy.wisc.edu/files/aihpAC8.pdf (accessed November 7, 2009). An advertisement for Godfrey's Cordial appears, in of all places, at the end of "The Behaviour, Confessions, and Dying Words, of the Malefactors, Who Were Executed at Tyburn, on Wednesday the 23d of this Instant December, 1730," *Ordinary's Accounts* for December 23, 1730, in *The Proceedings of the Old Bailey, 1674–1913,* online at http://www.oldbaileyonline.org/ (accessed November 7, 2009). Edward M. Brecher mentions the remarkable quantities of Godfrey's Cordial and other elixirs consumed in both Britain and the United States in "Nineteenth-Century America—A 'Dope Fiend's Paradise,'" a chapter in *The Consumers Union Report on Licit and Illicit Drugs* (Boston: Little, Brown, 1972), online at the Schaffer Library of Drug Policy, http://www.druglibrary.org/ (accessed November 7, 2009). Kalm's account appears in his *Travels in North America,* which I read in Adolph B. Benson's 1937 translation, *The America of 1750: Peter Kalm's Travels in North America* (New York: Wilson-Erickson, 1937). Safrole's evils are outlined in "Safrole, CAS No. 94–59–7," *Substance Profiles, Report on Carcinogens,* eleventh edition (National Toxicology Program, Department of Health and Human Services), online at http://ntp.niehs.nih.gov/ntp/roc/eleventh/profiles/s159safa.pdf (accessed November 7, 2009). Several writers mention sassafras's drug role in *Ecstasy: The Complete Guide,* edited by Julie Holland (Rochester, Vt.: Park Street Press, 2001), online at http://books.google.com (accessed November 7, 2009). Z. L. Nie, J. Wen, and H. Sun write about the "Phylogeny and biogeography of *Sassafras* (Lauraceae) disjunct between eastern Asia and eastern North America," *Plant Systematics and Evolution* 267 (September 2007).

Briar Patch

Darwin discusses thorn-bearing plants in an August 7, 1868 letter to G. H. Lewes included in *More Letters of Charles Darwin*, edited by Francis Darwin and A.C. Seward (London: John Murray, 1903), online at http://www.gutenberg.org/ (accessed November 7, 2009). Wallace wrote "On the Origin of Spines" in his 1889 *Darwinism: An Exposition of the Theory of Natural Selection*, online at http://www.gutenberg.org (accessed November 8, 2009). Henslow proposes his theory in *The Origin of Plant Structures by Self-Adaptation to the Environment* (London: Kegan Paul, Trench, Trübner, 1895), online at http://books .google.com (accessed November 7, 2009). Lamarck proposed his theories regarding acquired characteristics in his 1809 *Philosophie zoologique ou exposition des considérations relatives à l'histoire naturelle des animaux* (Zoological Philosophy, or An Exposition of Considerations Relating to the Natural History of Animals). Stephen J. Gould argues in "Shades of Lamarck," an essay reprinted in *The Panda's Thumb* (New York: Norton, 1992), that we have grossly over-simplified Lamarck's ideas. You can visit the Creation Museum electronically at http://www.creationmuseum.org (accessed November 7, 2009).

Hedges

The United States Department of Agriculture's PLANTS Database, online at http:// plants.usda.gov/index.html (accessed November 7, 2009), lists boxwood species growing in the United States. Colonial Williamsburg's online site, http://www.history.org (accessed November 7, 2009), positively describes Shurcliff's landscaping, while Edward A. Chappell questions it in his "The Museum and the Joy Ride: Williamsburg Landscapes and the Spectre of Theme Parks," in *Theme Park Landscapes: Antecedents and Variations*, edited by Terence G. Young and Robert B. Riley (Washington, D.C.: Dumbarton Oaks, 2002), online at http://books.google.com (accessed November 7, 2009). James R. Cothran mentions Bartram and quotes Price in *Gardens and Historic Plants of the Antebellum South* (Columbia: University of South Carolina Press, 2003), online at http:// books.google.com (accessed November 7, 2009). Michaux describes privet and roses in *Flora boreali-americana* (Paris, 1803), online at http://books.google.com (accessed November 7, 2009). The Georgia resolution is quoted in "Georgia State Flower," at NET STATE.com, online at http://www.netstate.com (accessed November 8, 2009). Gavin Menzies's *1421: The Year China Discovered the World* (New York: William Morrow, 2003) proposes that "Chinese ships had reached America seventy years before Columbus and circumnavigated the globe a century before Magellan." Carl Peter Thunberg, a Swedish naturalist and student of Linnaeus, collected plants in South Africa, Japan, and Ceylon. You can read his impression of Japan in a 1796 French translation *Voyages de C. P. Thunberg, au Japon, par le Cap de Bonne-Espérance*, online at http://www.google.com/ (accessed November 8, 2009). U.S. Fish and Wildlife Service agent Durward Allen recommended multiflora rose hedges in "Hunter Management with Multiflora Rose," *Journal of Wildlife Management* 12 (July 1948), as did Wallace L. Anderson and Frank C. Edminster in *Multiflora Rose for Living Fences and Wildlife Cover*, leaflet 256 (U.S. Department of Agriculture, 1949).

Vegetable Armature

Daniel H. Janzen and Paul S. Martin, in "Neotropical Anachronisms: The Fruits the Gomphotheres Ate," *Science* 215 (January 1, 1982), online at http://fusion.sas.upenn .edu/caterpillar/files/related/Janzen,1982anachronisms.pdf (accessed November 7, 2009), discuss megafaunal influence on seed dispersal, a theme popularized by, among others, Connie Barlow's *The Ghosts of Evolution: Nonsensical Fruit, Missing Partners, and Other Ecological Anachronisms* (New York: Basic Books, 2000). Both the Chinese and Japanese honey locusts were named *horrida*, the first by Karl Willdenow and the second by Carl Peter Thunberg, though today they are known, respectively, as *Gleditsia sinensis* and *G. japonica*, as mentioned in David More and John White's *The Illustrated Encyclopedia of Trees* (Portland, Oregon: Timber Press, 2003), online at http://books.google.com (accessed November 8, 2009). Jefferson refutes Buffon in his 1781 *Notes on the State of Virginia*, online at http://etext.virginia.edu/toc/modeng/public/JefVirg.html (accessed November 7, 2009). *Charles Willson Peale's Museum* (Academy of Natural Sciences), online at http://www.ansp.org/museum/jefferson/otherPages/peale__museum.php (accessed November 7, 2009), and Thomas O. Jewett, "Thomas Jefferson Paleontologist," *Early America Review* 3 (Fall 2000), online at http://www.earlyamerica.com/review/ 2000__fall/jefferson__paleon.html (accessed November 7, 2009), both weigh in on the controversy.

Mosquitoes

Charles Dickens's sour appraisal of Cairo, Illinois, occurs in his 1842 travel book, *American Notes*, available in any number of editions, including Project Gutenberg's, online at http://www.gutenberg.org (accessed November 7, 2009). Rebel firebrand Edmund Ruffin's *An Essay on Calcareous Manures*, third edition (Petersburg, Va.: printed for the author, 1842) is available online at http://books.google.com (accessed November 7, 2009). Adams and Franklin's amusing set-to is recounted in the four-volume *Diary and Autobiography of John Adams*, edited by L. H. Butterfield (Cambridge, Mass.: Harvard University Press, 1964). Edward John Waring's warnings regarding quinia come from *A Manual of Practical Therapeutics* (Philadelphia: Lindsay & Blakiston, 1866), online at http://books.google.com (accessed November 7, 2009). John Gerard's 1597 *Great Herball, or General Histoire of Plantes*, was one of the first comprehensive works on plants in English. He is widely used by later writers, and his terming sassafras the "ague tree" is quoted in J. K. Crellin, Jane Philpott, and A. L. Tommie Bass's *Herbal Medicine Past and Present: A Reference Guide to Medicinal Plants* (Durham, N.C.: Duke University Press: 1997), online at http://books.google.com (accessed November 8, 2009). Information on Maury's use of sunflowers to reduce malaria comes from Charles P. Russel's article, "Malaria," in *Popular Science Monthly* 9 (May–October 1876), online at http://books .google.com (accessed November 7, 2009). I quote Downing's comment about ailanthus trees in "Shade-Trees in Cities" (*Rural Essays*, New York: R. Worthington, 1856) in my *Aliens in the Back Yard* (Columbia: University of South Carolina Press, 2005). George Perkins Marsh's *The Earth as Modified by Human Action* (New York: Scribner, Armstrong, 1874), online at http://books.google.com (accessed November 7, 2009), mentions the salubrious climate of the Great Dismal Swamp, while Francis Porcher remarks on the electrical nature of pine trees in his *Resources of the Southern Fields and Forests, Medical, Economical, and Agricultural* (Charleston, S.C.: Evans & Cogswell, 1863), online at http:// docsouth.unc.edu/imls/porcher/porcher.html (accessed November 7, 2009). I discuss the rise and fall of the ailanthus in my *Aliens in the Back Yard* (Columbia: University of South Carolina Press, 2005).

Spring Ephemerals

A popular introduction to spring wildflowers of the area is Oscar Gupton and Fred Swope's *Wildflowers of the Shenandoah Valley and Blue Ridge Mountains* (Charlottesville: University Press of Virginia, 1979). The Virginia Native Plant Society has an online flower guide at http://www.vnps.org (accessed November 7, 2009).

Flying Frass

The "Aphides" article in the eleventh edition of the *Encyclopædia Britannica* gives a still-accurate overview of aphids. The eleventh edition is online at http://www.archive.org/ index.php (accessed November 7, 2009), and Wikipedia's aphid entry uses it, online at http://en.wikipedia.org/wiki/Aphid (accessed November 7, 2009). Pliny's musing on honeydew comes from his "The Qualities of Honey" in his *Natural History*, translated by John Bostock and H. T. Riley (London: Henry G. Bohn, 1855), online at http://books .google.com (accessed November 7, 2009). Murray makes his supposition in *A Treatise on Atmospherical Electricity* (London: Whittaker, Treacher & Arnot, 1830), online at http:// books.google.com (accessed November 7, 2009). Martha Weiss discusses scatapulting in her article "Good Housekeeping: Why Do Shelter-Dwelling Caterpillars Fling their Trass?" in *Ecology Letters* 6 (2003), online at Weiss's Web site, http://www9.georgetown .edu/faculty/emc26/MarthaWeiss/weissm/ (accessed November 7, 2009).

My Civil War

James I. Robertson Jr. raises Jackson and Junkin's thwarted love and Lewis's association with Jackson in *Stonewall Jackson: The Man, the Soldier, the Legend* (New York: Macmillan Library Reference, 1997). Miller's application for a Virginia pension is viewable online at the Library of Virginia, http://lva1.hosted.exlibrisgroup.com/F?RN=57900108 (accessed November 7, 2009). Doug Harwood writes about both Miller and the fate of Evergreen Cemetery's predecessor in articles in his monthly newspaper, the *Rockbridge Advocate*. An online source for the cemetery's fate is Eddie Dean's article, "The Black and the Grey," *Washington City Paper*, July 17, 1998, online at http://www.37thtexas.org/html/ Wshcitypaper.html (accessed November 7, 2009).

Migration

Kenneth Brugger's contribution to monarch butterfly studies is mentioned in the online *Encyclopædia Britannica* article on Brugger, online at http://www.britannica.com/ (accessed November 7, 2009). Lincoln P. Brower explains the multigenerational migration in "Monarch Butterfly Orientation: Missing Pieces of a Magnificent Puzzle," *Journal of Experimental Biology* 199 (1996), online at http://jeb.biologists.org/ (accessed

November 7, 2009). The online Paleoportal, http://www.paleoportal.org/ (accessed November 7, 2009), has a wealth of easily understandable entries about ancient geology, including one on the equatorial location of North America during the Ordovician.

Running the River

The *Field Guide to the Chessie Nature Trail* (Buena Vista, Va.: Mariner, 2009) has several fascinating articles regarding what was once a canal path and then a railroad between Lexington and Buena Vista. Bruce Terrell's *The James River Bateau: Tobacco Transport in Virginia*, East Carolina University Research Report No. 7 (1992), presents an overview of the development of the James River Canal and the 1983 discovery of bateaux built for the Virginia tobacco trade. Leland D. Baldwin's *The Keelboat Age on Western Waters* (Pittsburgh: University of Pittsburgh Press, 1941) includes the reference to Jefferson's bateau as well as other lore. William Trout's *An Automobile Tour and Field Guide to the North River Navigation* (Lexington, Va.: Rockbridge Historical Society, 1983) describes the canal from Lexington to the James River, while the Virginia Canals and Navigation Society's *The Maury River Atlas: Nineteenth-Century Inland Navigations of the Virginias* (Lexington, Va.: The Society, 1991) describes both the canal's remains downriver from Lexington and furnace- and bateau-traffic remains upriver.

Hay Bales

Alan Ritch has compiled an amazing online inventory of paintings and poems at his *Hay In Art* Web site, http://www.hayinart.com/ (accessed November 7, 2009). McCormick's reaper is discussed at the Shenandoah Valley Agricultural Research and Extension Center's McCormick Farm Web site, http://www.vaes.vt.edu/steeles/mccormick/mccormick .html (accessed November 7, 2009). *Core Historical Literature of Agriculture* (*CHLA*), from Cornell University's Albert R. Mann Library, contains thousands of nineteenth- and twentieth-century agricultural texts, including Cyrus McCormick's *The Century of the Reaper* (New York: Houghton Mifflin, 1931), online at http://chla.mannlib.cornell.edu/c/ chla/ (accessed November 7, 2009). The title of Follett L. Greeno's alternative history of the reaper indicates his fervor: *Obed Hussey, Who, of All Inventors, Made Bread Cheap; Being a True Record of His Life and Struggles to Introduce His Greatest Invention, the Reaper, and Its Success, as Gathered from Pamphlets Published Heretofore by Some of His Friends and Associates, and Reprinted in This Volume, Together with Some Additional Facts and Testimonials from Other Sources* (Rochester, N.Y.: Rochester Herald Publishing, 1912), available online at http://www.gutenberg.org (accessed November 8, 2009). Rodney B. Swift's *Who Invented the Reaper? An Answer to the Protest Statement Said to Have Been Filed at the Treasury Department* (Chicago, 1897), occasioned by a protest against placing McCormick's face on a new banknote, is blessedly shorter, pro-McCormick, and available online at http://www.archive.org/index.php (accessed November 8, 2009). Wikipedia provides an introduction to the Haymarket Affair, May 1, and Labor Day at http:// en.wikipedia.org/wiki/Main__Page (accessed November 7, 2009). It's worthwhile to contrast the Department of Labor's bland *History of Labor Day*, online http://www.dol .gov/OPA/ABOUTDOL/LABORDAY.HTM (accessed November 7, 2009), with PBS's more political *Origins of Labor Day*, online at http://www.pbs.org/newshour/bb/business/september96/labor__day__9–2.html (accessed November 7, 2009).

Sexual Swarms

Leks are a staple of animal-behavior texts, including Olivia Judson's *Dr. Tatiana's Sex Advice to All Creation: The Definitive Guide to the Evolutionary Biology of Sex* (New York: Holt, 2003). Audubon's comments come from his *Birds of America,* which came out in various editions over the years. The National Audubon Society has an online version of the 1840 edition at http://www.audubon.org (accessed November 7, 2009). Francis Drake writes of synchronous fireflies in "The Second Circum-Navigation of the Earth," *Hakluytus posthumus, or, Purchas his Pilgrimes*, volume 2, by Samuel Purchas (Glasgow: James MacLehose, 1905), online at http://books.google.com (accessed November 7, 2009). The *New York Times* ran an article, "Cannibalism among the Fireflies" (Science Watch, November 8, 1983), addressing the issue of predatory fireflies, and Matt Wasson wrote "The Synchronous Fireflies of Elkmont" for *Appalachian Voices* (June 2004), online at http://www.appvoices.org (accessed November 7, 2009). The Virginia Department of Game and Inland Fisheries describes the endemic Peaks of Otter salamander (*Plethodon hubrichti*) at its online site, http://www.dgif.virginia.gov/wildlife/information/?s=020039 (accessed November 7, 2009). Bryan D. Neff shows that "Paternity and Condition Affect Cannibalistic Behavior in Nest-Tending Bluegill Sunfish" in *Behavioral Ecology and Sociobiology* 54 (September 2003), abstract online at http://www.springerlink.com (accessed November 7, 2009).

Index

About the Author

JOHN LELAND is the author of *Aliens in the Backyard: Plant and Animal Imports into America, ForeWord* magazine's 2005 Book of the Year for Popular Culture, and *Porcher's Creek: Lives between the Tides,* second-place winner in the 2003 competition for the Phillip D. Reed Memorial Award of the Southern Environmental Law Center. Leland is a professor of English at the Virginia Military Institute in Lexington.